Growing up in THE 1930s

RICHARD GRIMMOND

Published in Australia by Sid Harta Books & Print Pty Ltd,
ABN: 34632585293
23 Stirling Crescent, Glen Waverley, Victoria 3150 Australia
Telephone: +61 3 9560 9920, Facsimile: +61 3 9545 1742
E-mail: author@sidharta.com.au

First published in Australia 2023
This edition published 2024
Copyright © Richard Grimmond 2023
Cover design, typesetting: WorkingType (www.workingtype.com.au)

The right of Richard Grimmond to be identified as the Author of the Work has been asserted in accordance with the Copyright, Designs and Patents Act 1988.

All rights reserved. No part of this publication may be reproduced, stored in a retrieval system, or transmitted, in any form or by any means without the prior written permission of the publisher, nor be otherwise circulated in any form of binding or cover other than that in which it is published and without a similar condition being imposed on the subsequent purchaser.

ISBN: 978-1-922958-56-3

About the Author

Richard Grimmond was born in 1927. He is a retired principal of Finley and Port Macquarie high schools. Richard was a foundation member of the Port Macquarie Historical Society in 1956 and was Port Macquarie-Hastings Citizen of the Year in 2010. He was also a member of the Lions Club for forty-six years and awarded the Lions Club Melvin Jones Award in 2013.

Other titles by Richard Grimmond

I went with John Oxley: Celebrating Oxley's Bicentenary 1818 – 2018

Port Macquarie 1821: Celebrating the Bicentenary

Harriet's Boy

*Dedicated to my mother and father
for giving me wonderful memories*

Contents

Chapter 1	*My Earliest Memories*	1
Chapter 2	*My Parents*	53
Chapter 3	*The Great Depression*	77
Chapter 4	*School*	89
Chapter 5	*Sunday School*	129
Chapter 6	*Toys and Games*	141
Chapter 7	*Holidays*	155
Chapter 8	*Washing Day*	177
Chapter 9	*Shopping and other outings*	185
Chapter 10	*Our Identity Found*	207
Chapter 11	*Winding up the 1930s*	213
Epilogue		221

CHAPTER 1

My Earliest Memories

It is not often that you come across a ninety-six-year-old with a crystal-clear memory of his childhood. I consider myself such a person, so I hope to entertain and inform you of my experiences growing up in Newcastle, New South Wales, in the 1930s, thus keeping alive an era that otherwise may fade into the past.

I was born in July 1927 and I remember the 1930s very clearly. Just being born was very different in the 1930s. I can confidently assume that most young people reading this book were born in a hospital. All of my school friends were born at home with the help of a midwife.

I was brought into the world by a midwife named Dulcie Brown, who fortunately lived in Queens Road, Tighes Hill, the same street as my parents. Nurse Brown also brought my brother into the world five years later. For some reason she sent us each a beautiful book every Christmas right up until our teenage years. I wonder if she did this for everyone she delivered, or were we special?

My earliest memory is sitting in my highchair; I must

have been only two and a half or three years old. I distinctly remember pushing the mashed pumpkin under the curved edge of my plate with my curved-handled baby spoon so my mother would not see it. I did not like mashed pumpkin. I remember that the tray would hit my forehead as it was lifted up, so I had to duck under it.

My High Chair

My highchair was a very special highchair. The family story is that it was purchased for my father with my grandfather's deferred pay when he came home from the Boer War in 1900. It is a most elaborate highchair, made with pieces of wood turned on a lathe, as well as pieces known as 'candy turnings' at the back.

My father used it when he was a small child and it was then used for his brother and two sisters who followed him. After that it was used for me and my brother. My parents kept it and it was used for my three children. I kept it and passed it on to my daughter and it was used by my two grandsons. Eleven children have sat in this historic highchair.

It has been restored many times with the rattan cane woven seat replaced exactly as it was originally. It is now in the Port Macquarie Museum.

18 Queens Road, Tighes Hill

I still clearly remember my parents' house at 18 Queens Road, Tighes Hill, a suburb of Newcastle. It had a glassed-in verandah along the eastern side and the warm morning sun filled the room. We had a large table under the glass windows where I would draw and paint.

My maternal grandfather was a primary school teacher in the Newcastle area when my mother was a teenager. His family lived at Teralba, a lakeside suburb of Newcastle. My mother travelled daily to Newcastle High School, which was then on the hill behind the Hunter Street shops in the centre of Newcastle.

When the Spanish flu pandemic struck Newcastle in 1918, Mum would have been fifteen years old. The school was closed and she did not complete her Intermediate Certificate, which was a lifetime regret for her. However, she did enjoy her studies, particularly art, and I am sure that she passed that love of art on to me.

At a very early age, I remember having colouring pencils and boxes of watercolour paints. My mother held my hand to paint between the lines until I could do it myself. At age three I could colour in with pencils and use watercolour paints. I could mix colours; red and blue to make purple, and yellow and blue to make green. I also did 'water-washes' for skies, that is, mixing a light blue paint with water and keeping the paint moving with no brush marks.

My memory was reinforced years later when, to my embarrassment, my mother would display my many painting books to visitors, saying, 'Richard did these when he was three'.

When I was about five, I can remember that there was an advertisement in the *Newcastle Morning Herald* for a colouring-in contest. It was promoting a new product – a tinned fruit salad called Tropical Fruit Salad. There was a large drawing of a bowl of mixed fruits, which was to be coloured in by the contestants.

Mum said, 'Other kids would be using coloured pencils, use your paints!' So I did. I used bright colours.

When the ten winners were announced in the newspaper, my name was on top of the list. I was so excited; it was like winning the lottery. The prize was a voucher to give to the grocer for a free tin of Tropical Fruit Salad. It was the most delicious fruit salad I had ever tasted.

Dad made me a drawing-board. It was a piece of pine, slightly larger than foolscap paper. I had a supply of drawing paper because Mr Mabbit, our policeman boarder, brought home lots of foolscap paper from his work that was only used on one side. I drew every day and sometimes took my board down the road to a friend's house in William Street to draw for them, long before I went to school. I don't know if it was a natural ability, or resulted from my mother's encouragement, but I loved drawing.

My parents' house was a typical 1930s working-class family home with weatherboards and a corrugated-iron roof. It was virtually a square divided into four, with the two front rooms being the main bedroom and the dining room.

The front bedroom contained an oak bedroom suite, consisting of the bed, dressing table, wardrobe and pedestal. The pedestal was a small cabinet about eighteen-inches square and about two-feet-six-inches high. It contained the chamber pot and on top of it stood a large china wash bowl and a matching tall jug used to hold water for washing someone who was sick in bed. This was common and most people had one, although it was rarely used.

The two other rooms were the second bedroom and the kitchen. Across the back was a glassed-in verandah and the bathroom. The laundry and toilet were underneath the house because the house was built on a sloping block.

The ceilings were ten-feet high, which was standard then, and were made with heavily decorated plaster. The walls were plaster in the dining room and bedrooms, and the kitchen was lined with tongue-and-groove cypress pine, set at forty-five degrees on the lower half of the wall and varnished showing the brown, knotty grain.

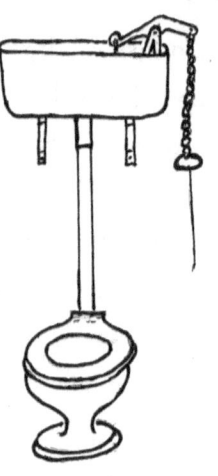

There was a flushing toilet downstairs. This was fairly modern, as the outer suburbs of Newcastle still had pans. Toilets were operated by pulling a chain attached to a high cistern, and all homes with children had a string or cord attached to the chain so small children could reach it.

Lights hung from the ceiling on cords about a yard long; they had white conical china shades covering the bare light bulbs.

Flies were a problem because fly screens were not common, so the kitchen light had flypaper attached. This was a length of sticky paper that caught flies by their wings or legs. Flypaper came in a small roll and when opened hung in a spiral for a couple of days before it straightened out.

Speaking of flies, milk jugs had to be covered with a white gauze material weighed down with beads, or sometimes seashells with holes in them, to keep the flies out of the milk.

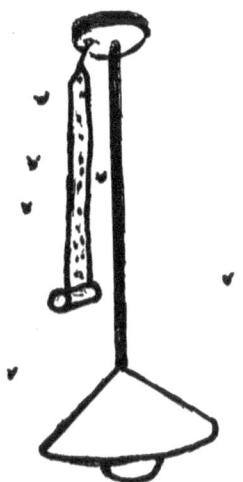

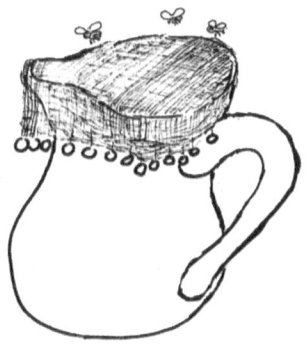

In the centre of the kitchen was a table. It was the hub of the house. Everything was done on the kitchen table: meal preparation and then the eating of meals, as well as the weekly cooking of cakes and biscuits, ironing, darning and sewing. Family board games were played at the kitchen table, and school homework was carried out. Dad read the paper on the table. On some occasions, bathing the baby took place on the kitchen table. It was certainly the centre of most family activities.

In the corner, at forty-five degrees to the walls, stood the cast-iron, black fuel stove, with a little coal box and small shovel on the hearth.

If the kitchen table was the hub of the house, then the stove would have been the focal point. It not only cooked all the meals but it provided warmth on a cold winter's night. The whole family would sit on the sofa placed in front of it, with the little door of the firebox open and the grate down horizontally so we could see the fire. Many a cold night was spent in front of the kitchen fire with my mother reading books to my brother and me.

I have fond memories of Monday nights, when two of my aunties visited us when Dad was working in the country. Auntie Jean and Auntie Nell, Mum's younger sisters, shared a flat in Watt Street near the beach in town. They both worked at Winn's, the big department store in Hunter Street.

Above the fireplace was the mantelshelf, which was the full width of the stove. Every home had one. A wind-up alarm clock stood on the mantelshelf by day and beside the bed at night. This clock signalled a very strict eight o'clock bedtime for children.

Chapter 1 My Earliest Memories

In the 1930s, every household had a set of canisters along the mantelshelf in the kitchen. This was a row of containers with labels; they decreased in size from the largest being FLOUR, then SUGAR, RICE, TEA, with the smallest canister being for COFFEE.

Also, every mantelshelf in the 1930s had the children's moneyboxes. In most homes this was a bright-red, cast-iron black boy, who put money in his mouth when it was placed on his hand. It was operated by a lever at the back. This most certainly would not be approved of these days.

The alternative was the pressed tinplate model of Sydney's Commonwealth Bank. I had the bank but my cousins had

the black boy. We were encouraged to save our pennies with the promise that we would be rich one day, so it was with pride and anticipation that we shook our heavy moneyboxes.

Above the mantelshelf in most Australian homes was a framed picture. We had a print of a painting of Lord Nelson's death at the Battle of Trafalgar. Dad said that it came from his mother's house in Minmi (an outer western suburb of Newcastle), and was from a Pears Soap advertising campaign. It was probably a reward for collecting a nominated number of wrappers, so hundreds of people would have had the same print.

Dad's mother had put it in a thick, black, old-fashioned frame. While being warmed in front of the fire, I had time to study every detail of that picture. I was intrigued by the huge sails, the cannons and the smoke of battle, as well as Lord Nelson lying on the deck with blood on his chest and the concerned expressions on the faces of those near him.

On the opposite wall to the stove stood the dresser. Most homes had a dresser in the kitchen. This was a piece of furniture that stood six feet tall. It had narrow shelves in the upper part and wider cupboards in the lower part. The shelves held the plates, which were stacked vertically. The large carving plate was in the centre and other plates were symmetrically placed each side.

The tablecloth and cutlery were stored in the two drawers, and food was kept in the cupboards below. The ends of the food cupboard were enclosed with sheet zinc, perforated with small holes for ventilation, a forerunner for screens.

Ants were always a problem, so the legs of the dresser often stood in saucers of water, but later, a pest control product called 'Dead Ant' was on the market. This was like two different sized small tins inside each other with a chemical inside them. The dresser stood on four of them and they kept the ants out.

The kitchen sink was in the corner of the kitchen. This was a deep, enamelled recess with a wooden draining board alongside it. Mum never used the wooden draining board; she always used a wash-up tray. In those days, before plastic draining racks, the washed dishes were leaned against an upside-down cup known as a 'leaner'. The person drying up knew not to dry that cup until last.

Speaking of washing-up reminds me that when collecting the dishes to be washed at the end of the meal, if a plate or piece of cutlery had not been used, it was hastily put aside or back in the cupboard with a smile and called a 'sunbeam'. It was funny to be visiting friends and hear another family call it a 'sunbeam' also. I think it was certainly a Newcastle expression, but it may have been a 1930s' expression in other Australian homes.

There was also the Newcastle custom of setting the breakfast table before going to bed. Our family did it for years, and I know all my aunties did it also. It was certainly a Newcastle custom; again, I don't know how far the custom spread.

Not only did Newcastle people set the breakfast table before going to bed, they always placed the porridge spoon, as well as the dessertspoon for other meals, across the top of each place at the table and at right angles to the knife and fork. All my relatives did this, and my wife Gwen said that when she was billeted with a Newcastle family on a school sports visit, that they did it also. Again, it was certainly a Newcastle custom, but may have been more widespread in the 1930s. It was not until I married Gwen that the dessertspoon went on the right-hand side.

Our wash-up tray had an image of the Sydney Harbour Bridge on it, as did thousands of others at 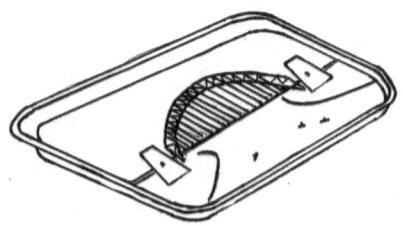 that time because we were all very proud of our newly opened Sydney Harbour Bridge in 1932.

There were pictures of the bridge on calendars, writing pads, chocolate boxes, trays, plates, magazines, badges, postage stamps (incidentally, the green five-shilling Harbour Bridge stamp is still one of Australia's most valuable stamps), matchbox covers, bookmarks, tea-towels, beach towels; in fact, everywhere you looked. I can remember every shop in town arranging their merchandise in the shape of the bridge. There was a model of the bridge in every shop window, including the chocolate shop, which had a six-foot model made of chocolate. The Harbour Bridge was a highlight in the midst of an economic depression.

We used that wash-up tray for years and years until the colour was completely worn away and it ended up a metal tray with a light-blue edge.

On the wall, between the sink and the dresser, was the family medicine cabinet. I must digress to explain home medicines in the 1930s. It cost ten shillings and sixpence or half a guinea (a seventh of a week's wages) to go to the doctor, so it was only in an extreme emergency that anyone went to the doctor. Home remedies were the order of the day.

Our medicine cabinet contained methylated spirits, the cure-all for cuts, scratches, rashes and pimples. It stung like hell, but we were assured that it killed germs. Another common remedy was eucalyptus oil. A few drops on a spoonful of sugar were ideal for a sore throat. Also, a few drops on a handkerchief announced to the whole classroom that you had a cold, but it was effective.

Then there was the Australian 'cure-all' of several drops of eucalyptus oil in a dish of near-boiling water and a towel over the patient's head with their face a few inches above the bowl. This was used for sore throats, stuffy heads, the common cold, and even the flu because it gave instant relief.

The cabinet also contained tweezers for splinters, a glass eye bath for rinsing eyes, and lots of rolled-up bandages of various sizes, made from old sheets. They were always washed and used again. They were mostly used for skinned knees, which seemed to be the most frequent accident with kids running around and chasing each other.

Incidentally, to fix the bandage in position, we did not use sticking plaster as one would today because it was too expensive. We would cut or tear the bandage horizontally for about a foot, and then tie a knot with the strips and use the two lengths to tie the bandage on firmly.

Castor oil was in the medicine chest for upset stomachs, which kids hated. There was also olive oil. I can remember a teaspoon of olive oil being heated with a lighted match under the teaspoon and poured into my ear to treat ear-ache. I screamed like an ancient warrior storming a castle. It was sheer torture.

Of course, we had Vicks VapoRub for rubbing on the chest for a cold. There were also the pink and purple packets of Aspro tablets for headaches. Some families used Bex or Vincents powders, but we always used Aspro; it must have been cheaper. We also kept the round blue tin of Rawleigh's Medicated Ointment for cuts and bruises. We even had Epsom Salts and Glauber Salts.

As if to lend weight to the authenticity of its contents, on the top shelf of the cabinet sat the black and silver St John Ambulance handbook. This was a little four-inch by five-inch textbook that Dad could recite from cover to cover. He attended the Railway first-aid classes for years and was awarded certificates; also bronze, silver and gold life-member medals.

The highchair stood under the medicine cabinet and a hot-water bottle hung on a hook behind it. The rubber hot-water bottle with its woollen cover was a great comfort in bed on a cold night, but if little feet touched the rubber under the cover, it was most painful.

Speaking of bedrooms reminds me of the chamber pot, or jerry as we called it. This was a china pot about twelve inches in diameter with a large handle  that stood under the bed and was used for urinating in at night. It was a carry-over from the 1920s, probably from our English ancestry. Even though we had a toilet downstairs, it avoided going outside at night or in the rain.

In the 1930s, many homes still had jerries under the bed. Of course, little boys had to kneel, and it gave an odour to the room, but this was accepted as normal in the 1930s.

In most bedrooms on summer nights, we had mosquito sticks. These were long, thin, green sticks about twelve inches long that fitted into a holder, although most homes stuck them into a piece of soap. As they burned, the sticks gave off a thick smoke that kept mosquitoes away; again, this was before fly screens on windows.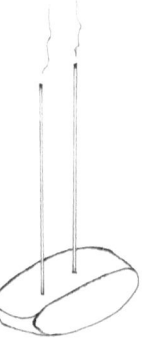

Many a time I went to sleep mesmerised by two red spots in the black night. Thicker mosquito coils came later.

Fly sprays evolved over the years. I remember early ones that were shaped like the letter 'T'. The long leg was placed in a bottle of fly spray and a person blew hard into the mouthpiece. This action drew liquid up the stem and converted it into a fine spray that came out the other end.

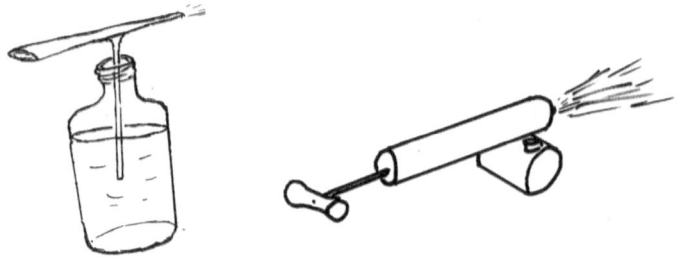

They were followed by a pump-action fly spray in which the liquid was held in a small cylinder. A piston was operated in a longer cylinder at right angles to the liquid container. This produced a fine spray that killed flies and mosquitoes.

Another innovation of the era was the butter-cooler. Only the very rich had refrigerators, and some people had ice chests, but ordinary working-class families used the butter-cooler. It consisted of two containers about nine

inches in diameter that were made of a porous plaster. They were soaked in a bucket of water for a while, then the two halves were put together with the butter inside. The process of evaporation took heat from its immediate surroundings and cooled the butter.

Keeping blowflies away from meat was always a problem, so most people had a meat safe. These were cube-shaped or cylindrical-shaped, made of perforated metal and hung in a cool place.

For a very short while, Mum had a Coolgardie safe, also called a drip safe. This was a homemade wooden frame, eighteen inches by eighteen inches and three-feet high with three-ply shelves, and it was covered with hessian. A dish of water was placed on the top with four pieces of flannel hanging over the side of the dish and down the sides of the safe. Water was absorbed by the woollen material and dripped down the four sides of the safe. Evaporation of the water from the hessian made the meat safe cool.

However, while it may have been satisfactory for the Western Australian gold miners in their dirt-floor tents, it made puddles on the floor that Mum was constantly cleaning up, so it was discarded.

Those people who had ice chests relied on the delivery of blocks of ice to keep their food cold. Dark's Ice Works in Newcastle had a fleet of horses and carts that delivered ice all over Newcastle. The large blocks of ice on the carts were covered with wet corn bags and were chopped into smaller blocks with an ice pick. They were carried into the customer's kitchen with ice tongs and placed inside their ice chest.

Children loved the 'iceman' because they gathered up the small chips from the ice being cut and sucked them. Hanging onto the back of the cart by their fingertips, and with legs swinging, they got a ride as the horse plodded to his next customer. I remember doing this often.

Most people kept water cool in a water bag. This was a rectangular canvas bag about a foot long with a stiff handle along the top edge and a white china spout. The water seeping through the canvas evaporated and cooled the water.

Water bags were hung in a cool place, usually in a draft.

There was always an enamel cup attached with a length of string. Some people attached their water bags to the front bumper bar of their cars, especially in the country. Of course, it would get caked in dust but the water was cool.

I can remember a round canvas water bag about a foot in diameter and about two-feet-six-inches high that hung on the platform at Hamilton Railway Station during the summer for the public to use. It had the usual enamel cup attached with a long cord to the handle and everyone used the same cup, but they always put about half an inch of water

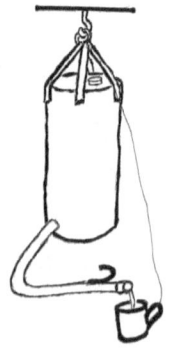

in it, swished it around and tossed it out, in an effort to clean it. This just would not happen these days. It had a long canvas tube with a white china spout. The tube was attached to the bottom of the water bag. There was no tap. When the tube was lowered the water ran out and after use it was hooked to the top of the water bag.

Speaking of cool drinks reminds me of 'fizzy drinks'. Before the era of Coca-Cola, we made our own carbonated drink with seltzer. It came as a white powder in a tin, and one heaped teaspoonful made a thirst quenching 'fizzy drink'.

Besides fizzy drinks, we sometimes had an orange drink. Mum would cut an orange in two, squeeze it on the glass-moulded orange squeezer to remove the juice and then add a little water and a spoonful of sugar. They were delicious. On special occasions, probably when Mum had an excess of eggs, we were given an egg flip. This was a beaten egg with some milk added. It always had brown nutmeg on top. In the wintertime, we often had a hot drink of Ovaltine going to bed. These were little luxuries that I remember with fondness. It was only at birthday parties and Christmas that we had 'bought' soft drinks.

We only had our meals in the dining room on special occasions. Our dining room was typical of the era and reflected attitudes of the times. It was the 'visitors' room'. Family rarely entered it unless parents were entertaining guests.

In our dining room there was a round oak dining table with chairs to match. Mum also had a Beale piano and a gramophone in this room. The upright piano was made from highly polished rosewood and there was a piano stool with a lift-up seat containing the music books.

The dining-room clock was a wedding present from

Mum's mother and father. It was made from highly polished rosewood and had a large round face with very classical-looking Roman numerals. The shape around the face extended outwards on each side, making the width of the clock about eighteen inches. It was an eight-day clock, which meant that it was wound once a week. Dad did this religiously every Sunday night before he went to bed. This clock also sat on the mantelshelf of the Islington house. We constantly referred to it for school time, as well as Sunday School time. Our lives were regulated by that clock, as well as by the Newcastle whistles.

Mum and Dad at the Islington House

Newcastle was unique in that the BHP whistles and the dockyard whistle could be heard just about throughout the entire inner Newcastle in those days. Locals set their clocks by them. There were whistles at the change of shifts at the steelworks at 8 am and 4 pm, as well as midnight. Then there was the deep drone of the dockyard whistle at 10 pm every night.

Our clock struck exactly as the whistles were blowing. It had a melodic strike on the hour, counting out the number of hours, with a single strike for the half hour. This went right through the night. Most dining room clocks struck on the hour but some gave a full chime on the hour, with a half chime for the half hour, a quarter chime for the quarter hour, and a three-quarter chime for quarter to the hour.

On a shelf over the fireplace stood a china ornament of the Three Wise Monkeys. One had its hands over its eyes, the next had hands over its mouth and the third had hands over its ears. The symbolism was that they saw no evil, spoke no evil, and heard no evil. I remember seeing the monkeys in other people's homes, so they were very common in the 1930s.

I must mention china rails and friezes, distinct features of the 1930s that seemingly came and went within that decade. A china rail was a narrow shelf that went completely around a dining room or living room, about two feet down from the ceiling. Special ornaments, mainly china plates, hence the name, were displayed on the rails.

A frieze was a brightly coloured wallpaper strip that was glued under the china rail, or picture rail if there was no china rail. This contrasted with the plain-coloured wallpaper and brightened the room. It was sometimes used in bedrooms as well.

There were a variety of floor coverings during the 1930s.

Firstly, linoleum was always popular, even in dining rooms. Old newspapers were always placed under the linoleum, or 'lino' as we called it, so the marks of the floorboards would not show through. This was years before we had floor sanders. I can remember the fun replacing worn lino years later and reading old newspapers, especially finding old *Ginger Meggs* comics from when they were printed on very large pages in the early 1930s.

Before we had carpeted floors, we had carpet squares. These had about two feet of floorboards showing around the edge that were stained dark-brown. Hallways had runners, which were carpet material, also with stained boards at the sides.

Floor coverings evolved throughout the 1930s, long before fitted carpet covering was common. We had linoleum in the Tighes Hill house and carpet squares in the Islington house.

Back to 18 Queens Road … on the other side of the fireplace stood the gramophone. It was typical of the day – three-feet high with an opening at the top and a cloth-covered speaker at the front. To operate it, we wound up the spring by turning a handle, and then carefully lowered the needle onto the record. Needles were steel and had to be frequently replaced.

Records were black and made of shellac, long before vinyl, and they operated at seventy-eight revolutions per minute. The names of the songs that I can remember are: *Sonny Boy*; *When your hair has turned to silver*; *Bye, bye, blackbird*; and *I don't work for a living*. I remember the line: 'I'll bet you I'll hang up that picture, if somebody drives the nail.' We were always amused by that one.

Mum played the piano and we often had visitors, as well as family, standing around the piano singing for hours. It was normal for those days. The singers stood behind the piano player to read the words of the songs from the music book. Dad was in a choir and had a good voice. He also played a banjo mandolin and a Jew's harp. A Jew's harp was a circular metal frame that fitted inside the player's mouth while he flicked a central spring-like reed, emitting a note that could be varied by shaping the player's mouth.

Some of the songs that we sang in the 1930s were: *Ye banks and braes o' Bonnie Doon*; *Little brown jug*; *Two little girls in blue*; *I'll walk beside you*; *You take the high road*; *Daisy, Daisy*, and many more. There was no 'top of the current charts', they were just old favourites. Then, of course, at Christmas time we went through all the carols, including *Silent night* and *Away in a manger*, as well as Christmas songs such as *Jingle bells* and *Good King Wenceslas*.

There was always supper after the singing. Mum's specialty was sausage rolls. They were very pleasant memories.

Other family activities included board games. I can remember playing Snakes and Ladders as well as Steeple Chase, which was a horse race game, with players throwing a dice to advance a number of places according to the throw of the dice to be the eventual winner. The family had many nights playing board games when I was growing up. I can also remember playing dominoes.

We played table tennis in the glassed-in back verandah. Dad bought a set of rope quoits and fixed a steel post into a block of wood and we played quoits with the family.

We also had a game called Bobs. This was played with a cue and a set of wooden balls a bit smaller than billiard balls. Someone must have given it to us; I am sure Mum would never have purchased it.

The Bobs game had a wooden frame with a row of nine archways with numbers above them, and two side arms to prevent the balls falling off the table. The object of the game was to hit the balls into the numbered arches after they had contacted the red ball that stood on a 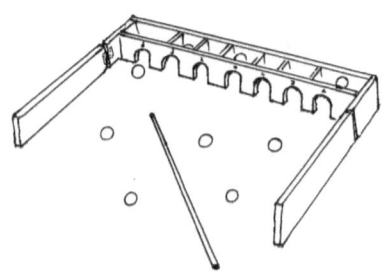 designated marked spot in front of the archways. The winner had the highest score when the numbers on the archways with balls inside were totalled.

We never owned a set of fiddlesticks, but sometimes when we were visiting another family, their children had them and the children played while the parents talked. The game consisted of about fifty thin sticks, a foot long, probably bamboo and coloured dark-green and red. They had pointed ends somewhat like knitting needles. The sticks were bunched together by hand, stood vertically on the table, then allowed to fall into an untidy heap. The object of the game was for a player to remove as many sticks as possible without disturbing other sticks. House rules varied; some rules allowed each player to take one stick each in turn until they moved another stick, then they were out. The score being the number of sticks removed.

A second way of playing the game was for one player to remove as many sticks as possible until others moved then they were out and the next player gathered up the sticks and allowed them to fall again.

We also played table tennis with a balloon, using our hands for bats, and soccer with opposing teams blowing a balloon on the table-tennis table. There were not many scores but lots of laughs.

Without TV in the 1930s, families entertained themselves with games and other group activities.

༺ ༻

In our Tighes Hill house, the pattern of daily life was focused around the kitchen. The morning began by emptying the stove ashes from the day before. This entailed Dad making a quick trip downstairs with the full ashtray to be emptied in a special place in the garden, and then collecting a handful of lighting sticks from the wood heap. With a page of old newspaper, the fire was set and a wax match was taken out of the small cylindrical matchbox that always sat on the mantelshelf near the clock.

The blue head of the match was struck on the sandpaper bottom of the matchbox and the fire was on its way. When all the sticks were alight, fine coal was added slowly, and it was not long before the breakfast fire was blazing.

The first saucepan heated was always the milk, because without refrigeration for most people, the milk 'went off' quickly, and boiling prevented that. Just before it boiled it rose like a cauliflower and could spill over, so it was my job to watch the aluminium saucepan and call, 'Woop the milk!', and my mother would quickly lift the saucepan off the heat before it spilled onto the stove. One bonus of boiled milk was the thick layer of cream that formed on the surface as it cooled. This was collected and placed in a jam dish to be used later on top of a slice of bread and jam as a special treat.

In winter, the porridge was cooked while being stirred regularly. Granose, a precursor of Weet-Bix, was eaten for breakfast in the summer.

I must mention one of my favourite breakfasts. If there was a heel of stale bread left over and a new loaf was available, the stale bread was used for 'bread and milk'. The bread was cut into thick slices then cut both ways to make one-inch cubes and placed into a porridge bowl. Boiling water from the kettle was poured over the bread until it was completely saturated. A saucer was pressed down on it and it was drained over the sink. If it was for more than one person, the chopped bread was placed in a small basin with the same procedure. After the hot water was drained off, it was served in porridge bowls with milk and sugar added.

Chapter 1   My Earliest Memories

The porridge was followed by bacon and eggs, or poached eggs, or scrambled eggs, or boiled eggs. We had about six fowls, so there were always plenty of eggs. This was a saving because eggs were one shilling a dozen; that is, a penny each, and they remained at this price throughout my childhood. Boiled eggs were always eaten with 'soldiers', which were strips of toast, less than an inch wide, for dipping into the runny yellow yolk. Most kids loved them. While the eggs were cooking, it was my job to make the toast. This was done by opening the firebox door and lowering the grate. I rested a thick piece of bread on the grate and held it over the coals with a homemade wire toasting fork.

Everybody had a homemade toasting fork. This was made with two lengths of wire, a bit less than a yard in length, doubled in the centre and twisted together. This was done over a bolt in the vice, or any fixed support such as a nail in a piece of wood, until the shaft was stiffened with an even twist. The last four inches were shaped with pliers. One strand was twisted firmly around the other three, then the two outside pieces of wire were shaped with pliers to form the outside fork prongs and all three were snipped off level to form the fork.

Even cutting the bread was so different to today. There was no sliced bread, so every slice had to be cut from the loaf with a bread knife on a breadboard. It had its advantage in that thicker slices could be cut for toasting. Incidentally, bread was always kept in a bread tin, a special large container like a small bin with a lid and a label, 'BREAD'. In our kitchen, it stood on the floor.

The shape of the loaves was different in the 1930s. Bread came in two half loaves with rounded tops, not square like much of today's bread. They were joined in the centre so they could easily be pulled apart. A half loaf could be bought for threepence halfpenny or a full loaf for seven pence. The first slice was called the 'softie' and was always in demand.

Lunches were sometimes bread and banana. A banana was cut into many small circular slices and placed evenly over the bread. It was traditional that a light sprinkling of sugar coated the bananas to give them a crunch.

Sometimes we had bread and dripping. I have read that during the Depression, people were reduced to eating bread and dripping through necessity. I would hope that our bread and dripping was not an economy measure but rather a novelty, because I liked it, particularly when it was flavoured with the fat from the Sunday roast dinner.

Bread and Golden Syrup was always popular, as was honey. Of course, we always had a jam open, and there was packet cheese and a jar of Marmite (long before Vegemite replaced it). So, we had plenty of variety with our lunches when I was growing up at Tighes Hill. In the 1930s, children were often told to eat the crusts as they were supposed to make their hair curly.

On cooking days, when I was very young, I always made

a pastry man for Dad. I can remember making the shape of a man about four inches long, with arms and legs and three small currants down his chest for buttons, as well as two for eyes. Any discolouration I think came from soot in the stove but Dad always asked if I had washed my hands.

The cast aluminium kettle was always 'singing' at the back of the stove; that is, it was just kept at boiling point but not boiling vigorously. When boiling water was required, the kettle was pulled forward over the fire for a few minutes. Everyone kept a glass marble inside their kettle so that its movement, when the water was boiling, kept the bottom of the kettle free from limescale that deposited inside kettles.

The family finished every meal with a cup of tea. The children had milk. There were two breakfast times on school days: the first just before Dad left for work, and then breakfast before school.

Weekends had a different pace. Saturday and school holiday lunches were mainly bread with banana or Golden Syrup. Some families called Golden Syrup, 'Cocky's Joy', but we never did.

Saturday lunches in the cooler months often included saveloys. These were red-skinned, shaped like sausages, and were boiled. They were always a favourite, as were their smaller versions called frankfurters.

Other Saturday quick lunches were baked beans, spaghetti, rissoles, and sometimes tripe or sheep brains in breadcrumbs, or even a scrambled or poached egg. Our lunches had plenty of variety, and we loved them.

Sunday's midday meal was always a baked dinner. After hours of shelling peas, stringing beans and peeling potatoes and pumpkin, the roast was coated in dripping (fat) and baked in the fuel stove. The smells were delicious. Then, of course, came the Yorkshire Pudding. It would not be a Sunday dinner without it. This was a tasty bread-like dish with a crispy crust that accompanied the roast.

Today, a popular meal in Australia is roast chicken; it is available everywhere. However, in the 1930s, 'poultry', as we called it then, was rare and we only had it on special occasions, such as Christmas or Easter. I remember the ritual of killing a 'chook', cleaning it and baking it for a special occasion. Firstly, one was selected among the fowls in the fowl yard, probably an old one or a bad layer. Then using a solid block of wood, and an axe, the head was chopped off and it was hung up by the legs on the clothesline for half a day to drain the blood out of it. Next, a kettle and a saucepan were boiled and the hot water was poured into the baby's bath on the back verandah table. Then began the smelly job of plucking all the feathers out, one at a time, while dipping it regularly into the near-boiling water.

If we thought that was unpleasant, the next step was absolutely disgusting. When the insides were cut out, the smell was revolting. These were flushed down the toilet. Next, the cavity was stuffed with stuffing, which included breadcrumbs, onion, celery, herbs and spices. For some unknown reason to a little boy, the legs were tied together with string. It was covered with fat and cooked in the oven for ages. The smells were

Chapter 1   My Earliest Memories

delicious. When ready, the cooked chook was placed on the big carving plate that always stood in the centre of the dresser. Incidentally, Mum always carved the chook and other roast meats, although at that time many husbands carved the meat. It was an English tradition. My grandfather always carved the meat but Dad always left it to Mum.

I have no need to tell you that the taste always matched the delicious smells, but as I said, a roasted fowl was a once-a-year event in the 1930s in our house and in many other homes also.

Mentioning the dinner table reminds me that I was taught table manners at an early age; that is, how to hold a knife and fork properly and how to eat small mouthfuls with my mouth closed. In fact, Mum did such a good job of teaching me table manners that when we went to other people's homes, they always commented on my good table manners. The same applied to my younger brother a few years later.

Besides table manners, we were expected to eat everything on the plate; we didn't have a choice. I have noticed that in recent generations, children have the option of finishing the meal, but that did not happen during Depression days. Every plate was left completely empty; there was no waste of food. That Depression attitude stuck with me for the whole of my life. I still leave a clean plate after every meal.

Another memory was jam-making. Most families made their own jam in the 1930s. It usually started with a friend having a fruit tree that was loaded with fruit, or simply when our grape vine over the fowl house had a good crop. The kitchen was turned into a mass production factory with dishes of fruit and piles of seeds and skins. It was not long before delicious smells were coming from the big pot on the stove. When sugar was added it seemed like tons to a small kid, then it was stirred continually.

After the jam cooled down the jars were filled. Sealing the jam jars changed dramatically over the years. Initially, I remember my mother melting wax and pouring the molten wax in the top of each jar. Then later on this was replaced with little squares of cellophane dipped in vinegar and secured with a rubber band. Of course, all the jars had to be labelled with the name of the jam and the date. Then the cupboards were stacked and gloated over, like money in the bank. Special friends and family were given a jar of jam.

Other early memories are of our boarder, a policeman named Mr Mabbit. My mum was a wizard handling money, as I shall point out many times in this story. In the early 1930s we had a spare bedroom and Mum could see its potential for earning an income, so we took in a boarder, which meant that I was sleeping in the cot in the front bedroom until I was four. I remember that, too.

The extra income meant that Dad bought a

Harley-Davidson motorbike and sidecar. It was our pride and joy. It was second-hand and had one small dent on the petrol tank. The previous owner had had a spill and was pleased to be rid of it, so Dad purchased it for thirty-eight pounds (I found on the internet that, in 2015, the same model sold in the USA for $600,000). Dad sold ours for fifty pounds after World War II and was well pleased. We went everywhere on it – shopping on Friday nights, to the beach on Saturdays, and visiting family.

The Harley had a foot clutch operated with the left foot and hand gears changed by moving a knob on a lever along the left side of the petrol tank. The accelerator functioned by turning the right handlebar grip. The brake was operated with the right toes and the ratchet brake was applied with the right heel to hold the bike on a hill. Incidentally, the 1927 black Harley-Davidson police bike had a reverse gear for crowd control.

Our Harley was the traditional khaki colour with the red and black pinstriping design around the edges. It was my job to clean the rims every Sunday morning when Dad washed it, so I remember it well.

I must tell you about buying petrol. There were no single-brand petrol stations like there are today. The customer had a choice from a row of pumps, all with different names. There was Plume with the big purple feather on the pump, as well as Atlantic in its red, white and blue colours, and Shell, in yellow and red colours.

And, would you believe, it was the bowser attendant, and

not the customer, who unscrewed the petrol cap and put the hose in the tank? He would then pump a long handle back and forth to fill the glass container at the pump with one gallon or two gallons as required. He then released a valve and gravity ran the petrol into the tank. Before he asked for the money, he opened the bonnet and checked the oil and water, adding some if needed. And with brisk efficiency, he checked all the tyres and added air if necessary. One shilling and nine pence a gallon, which based on today's prices is under five cents a litre!

We always went to 'Peter's Corner', just out of Mayfield. For buying a full tank, we received a free packet of Wrigley's PK chewing gum. How times have changed since the 1930s.

Dad and Ted Mabbit often went to the Newcastle beach in the Harley on a Saturday morning for a swim. They always took me with them, and when we came home, I would hose the salt water off them in our backyard. Mr Mabbit had a Kodak Baby Brownie box camera and Mum took a photograph of me hosing them.

Mr Mabbit rode a black 1927 Harley-Davidson and sidecar for the police force, so he had policeman's leather leggings. For some reason, he dressed me in his police leggings and took my photo in various poses. I can still remember sitting and standing on the clothes box as if it were yesterday. I guess seeing the photographs frequently kept my memories alive. I remember how uncomfortable it was, because I could not bend my knees and had to walk stiff-legged for the photographs. Luckily, we have kept the set of photos for

Chapter 1 My Earliest Memories

Me hosing Dad and Mr Mabbit

Me posing in Mr Mabbit's police leggings

over ninety years and I am able to include them in my book. The box with holes in it was Mum's laundry basket that Dad had made for her, and the photographs were taken in the back yard of 18 Queens Road when I was three years old.

When my brother was born in 1932, he had the cot, so I moved to the second bedroom and we lost our boarder.

Another early memory of the 1930s was making a telephone call. This will certainly surprise the mobile phone users of today. When my mother wanted to telephone her sister, my Auntie Jean, who lived in the centre of Newcastle, she had to walk several blocks across Tighes Hill to the public telephone box on a corner of William and Elizabeth Streets near the shops. I did not know anyone who had a phone in their house. My auntie lived in a boarding house and there was a telephone for the landlady. The boarders had to pay for each call that they made, of course.

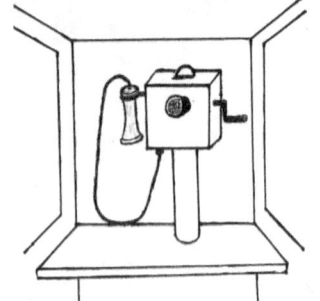

Firstly, my mother had to vigorously turn a small handle to alert the operator, who would ask, 'Number, please?' After my mother gave the four-digit number verbally there was a slight pause, then the operator said, 'Insert two pennies in the slot and press the button'.

After my mother had put in two pennies and pressed the button, the operator would hear them fall. She would then say, 'Go ahead, please,' and Mum was able to talk to my auntie

Chapter 1 My Earliest Memories

through a conical black funnel while holding the ear piece to her ear, which was attached to the phone with a long cord. I would be lifted up onto the shelf and I would say a few words to Auntie Jean. After a brief conversation, Mum hung the receiver on a hook and that terminated the call.

There is another early memory that I can recall clearly; it was when I had my photograph taken at a professional studio. When I was four, my mother and I travelled to Campsie, a suburb in Sydney, to have my photograph taken. The professional photographer was my grandfather's sister-in-law. I was asked to pose with my hand on my shoe. I remember at the time thinking it might be dirty on my hand but it looked all right in the finished product.

Mum was proud of that photograph. She gave copies to my grandparents and all my aunties, and she had a coloured enlargement mounted in a large oval frame that hung in the living room for years. It seemed an extravagance in Depression times. Mum must have been given a very large discount.

Another early memory of living at Tighes Hill was the interaction with the kids in the street. In those days before preschools, social integration was just mixing with the neighbours. Queens Road had about twelve boys and girls ranging in age from five to thirteen.

Every evening, especially during the long summer twilights, we would all play in the street in front of the houses. As soon as a few voices were heard, they attracted others and it was not long before all the kids in the street were out playing together; something not seen these days.

Studio photograph of me at age four

Evening was playtime on the road because there were no cars and all the horse and cart deliveries were over so we had the gravel street to ourselves for cricket, rounders (baseball with a broom stick) or, most popular, Red Rover All Over. We also played Release, a chase and catch game. We even played the English game, Oranges and Lemons. This was a game where the two people organising the game, usually the two oldest girls, stood facing each other holding hands. They began to sing, *Oranges and lemons*, and the others would form a long line and join in the singing, passing between the two girls holding hands. They would raise their arms and enclose the player's head, then move on to the next person while singing, *... the bells of Saint Clements* (I'm sure we said Saint Clemonds to rhyme with lemons, but the English version is St Clements). *When shall I pay you? Today or tomorrow. Chippachoppa; chippachoppa; last man's head, head, head ... OFF!* Then their arms would come down and enclose the player's head. The person who was caught with the word 'off' was taken aside and given the choice of two different things offered by each of the 'choppers'. Whichever choice was selected determined the particular chopper they stood behind. The winning chopper would have the longest queue of players behind him or her at the end of the game. The choices varied each game from a chest full of precious jewels, to bars of gold, depending on the organiser's imagination. This is the Tighes Hill way of playing the game. I believe that in the original English version, the choice was oranges or lemons. That makes sense, but trust the Aussies to give it their own twist. However, as unusual as it seems now, it was popular with the Queens Road kids in the 1930s. As it became dark and street lights came on, one by one we would hear a mother's voice calling a name, 'Thomas!' or 'Phillis!' and that person would leave the group until there were none left.

In every household it would be the same, 'Wash those

feet before you go to bed!' because everyone played in bare feet, even the girls. A big dish was placed in front of a chair or the sofa and feet were washed in cold water. Sometimes it was warmed with a slurp from the kettle. Feet were dried with a 'bag-towel'. Every home had a bag-towel. This was an opened-out sugar bag, trimmed with bias binding around the edge, which is a colourful ribbon of material with the weave at forty-five degrees. The bag-towel would be softened after a few times being boiled in the copper, and ours always hung on a hook inside the door of the saucepan cupboard under the sink, where it was available to dry wet hands quickly. Mum often wore a bag-apron, especially on washing days. This was an apron also made from an opened and washed sugar bag with colourful bias binding around the edges and the pocket.

But I digress ... another group activity for 'the street kids' of Queens Road was sailing toy boats on the 'flats' at high tide on the weekends. Actually, we pulled them along with string. In those days there were mudflats between King Street and the road to the Carrington 'tip'. This was an area as big as four football fields that filled with water about knee deep in the spring tides. The water came from Throsby Creek through a cement drain about a yard square and fifty yards long through the mud then under the road to Carrington, an extension of Elizabeth Street, to fill the 'flats'.

One Sunday morning, we were holding our boats in the swift current when Johnny Hadfield, who was between three and four years old, toppled in and was swept into the square cement drain. He was pulled out by the out-going tide. We could see his head disappearing down the drain with about a foot of headroom. His brother, Tommy Hadfield, seven or eight years old at the time, ran the full length of the cement drain. He laid on his stomach at the end and could see the little head bobbing down the drain. As Johnny came out of the end and into Throsby Creek, Tommy caught him and pulled him out. They would be old men now, if they are still alive. If they are, I wonder if they remember the day Tommy saved his brother's life?

Another memory of Queens Road is playing with the doctor's children. Doctor Brown, his wife and three children John, Louise and Margo, lived in Henry Street. The front of their big brick house actually overlooked Elizabeth Street above a high cliff but the entrance gate and tall brown fence faced Queens Road at the corner. I don't remember how I was invited to play with them. I probably looked a 'nice little boy' who wore shoes with socks held up with garters, and spoke nicely. I played with them most Saturday mornings and school holidays. I mention this story because it was a window into another world. It was literally 'how the other half lived' in the 1930s. The Browns had two adjoining blocks of land; the second one was mainly rose gardens and a drying lawn. They had two cars and two servants ... No, make that three: a nanny for the children, a housekeeper and a gardener. They insisted that the two female servants wore white starched uniforms. The Browns had their own golf putting green, a white-tiled bathroom, two toilets (one in the bathroom and one on the verandah) as well as two dogs.

They had a refrigerator and made their own ice-cream, which they ate from saucers with teaspoons. It was a new world for me. The children had a large sand pit and a doll's house that they could get inside.

Besides playing with the children, they often took me with them when they went out in one of the cars. The children sat in the 'dickie seat'. This was a seat at the back of the cabin that opened up to provide extra seating. We had the wind in our faces and could wave to people.

Mrs Brown played golf and her photograph was often in the *Newcastle Morning Herald*. It was certainly a different world to 18 Queens Road, and only a few houses away.

Another early memory is my grandfather's car; it was a 1927 Chevrolet. It was a very popular model and there was a very high percentage of 1927 Chevs on the roads in the 1930s. He was fortunate to own a car in Depression times. He was a teacher and had a regular government income.

The Chev was originally a grey-green colour but when he retired, my grandfather had it resprayed a light brown; it looked very smart. I was proud to  be driven in it. I must describe it for the car owners today. It was said to have a 'cloth top', which meant that it could be collapsed to make it open, but he never did. It had no side windows, only side 'curtains' that could be put up with press-studs in wet weather. I remember that the wheels had large wooden spokes. The car had a foot clutch and the gears were changed with a gear-stick standing up from the floor with a knob larger than a golf ball at the top. The self-starter was on the floor, but if the battery was flat then it was started with a crank handle at the front. There was one windscreen wiper that was manually operated with a little crank-handle at the top of the windscreen. The tail-light switch was outside the car and at twilight we had to stop the car and someone got out and ran around the back to turn it on. The Chev had no boot so the luggage was strapped onto the running boards, and there were no traffic indicators. My grandfather had to stretch his right arm horizontally out of the window to show that he was turning to the right. When stopping, he bent his elbow at ninety degrees and held his hand up outside the window. Compared with today it was primitive.

Before I leave my maternal grandfather, I must give you a thumbnail sketch of his interesting life. He was born in England and his father was a lead miner. When the Spanish began producing lead much cheaper than England, all the English lead mines closed and my grandfather's family migrated to Australia when he was four years old. The family came out on a steamship that also had sails. He told me that the images that remained in his mind were of the sails being covered with soot from the ship's funnels.

His father found work in a coal mine at Wallsend, near Newcastle. Unfortunately, he was killed in a fall of coal and is buried at Wallsend cemetery. My grandfather and his brothers were adopted by the Pomeroy family and his mother remarried. As a young man he studied through Blackfriars Correspondence College. While he was studying, he obtained work in the coal mine at Wallsend as the boy opening and closing the hessian curtain, called a brattice, which redirected airflow down the coal mines. His job was to draw back the curtain when he heard a train coming. The train was a truck full of coal, drawn by a pit pony. He told me that while he was sitting there between trainloads of coal, he studied by candlelight to be a teacher. He was successful, gaining the necessary qualifications and becoming a primary school teacher. He taught at many country schools over his lifetime. His last two schools were Timbumburi and Wallabadah, near Tamworth. When he retired, he built a house in Hamilton South, Newcastle, to be near family. I had a great affection and respect for my grandfather.

There is one memory of my grandfather that amuses me, and that was seeing him drink his tea from a saucer. Quite frequently, when his cup of tea was too hot, he tipped some into his saucer, and very carefully drank from it using two hands. Saucers seemed deeper then. Today it would be the height of bad manners, but in the 1930s it was apparently accepted as normal in a family situation because I have seen my uncles and my father also drink tea from a saucer when it was too hot to drink immediately. I remember admiring the skill of holding it perfectly level and not spilling it, and wondering if I could do it so well when I was a grown-up. The things we remember. Thank goodness the practice stayed in the 1930s.

Yet another early memory of the 1930s was seeing Charles Kingsford Smith's famous aeroplane, the *Southern Cross*. It was the first aeroplane to cross the Pacific Ocean. Kingsford Smith visited Newcastle Aerodrome in 1931 and my father took me and my cousin, Jack Attwood, in the Harley-Davidson to the aerodrome to see it. We walked right around it and I touched the wheel and the tail to say that I had actually touched the famous *Southern Cross*. We were in awe of it at the time. Looking back now, it was real history.

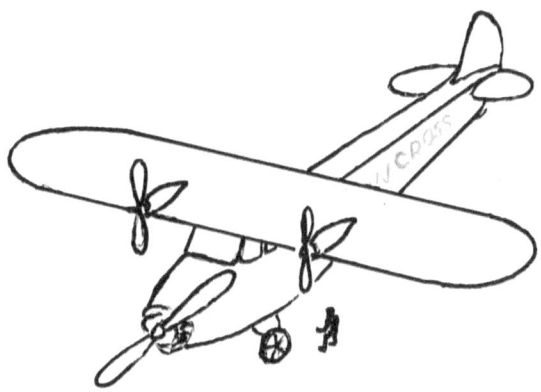

Southern Cross, 1931

Besides Kingsford Smith, there were other celebrities who won the hearts of people going through the Depression. When there was doom and gloom on the employment front, ordinary people had to look for something to brighten their lives and they found this through celebrities and events in the news, such as Don Bradman, Phar Lap, and Shirley Temple, to name a few.

Don Bradman, Australia's most famous cricketer, was everyone's hero. We were so proud of him that people stayed up late to hear the games in England; that is, those who had access to a wireless, as the radio was called in those days. Even in my own family, my brother was named Bruce Donald in honour of the famous man. The Methodists loved him because he did not drink alcohol, which was often quoted.

As well as Don Bradman, the whole country loved a racehorse called Phar Lap. He won the Melbourne Cup in 1930, when the whole country stopped what they were doing to listen on crackly wirelesses. This was a reaction to gloomy news all around them. When Phar Lap met his untimely death, the body was preserved in the Melbourne Museum and the heart was preserved in the Canberra Museum. I remember that as young children, my brother and I were taken to see both, which shows how highly regarded Phar Lap was at the time.

And then there was Shirley Temple, everyone's favourite child actress. She won the hearts of the old and young alike. Sound movies were in their infancy and, even in Depression times, people flocked to the 'pictures' to see Shirley Temple. Mothers dressed their daughters and curled their hair to copy the child actress. Many little girls were taught to tap dance because Shirley Temple tap danced.

Also, as a nation, everyone was proud of our capital, Canberra, and the fact that the whole city was designed by one man, Walter Burley Griffin. When the new parliament house was opened in 1927, a coin was issued to commemorate the event. It was affectionately known as the Canberra Two

Chapter 1   My Earliest Memories

Bob. As kids in the 1930s, we always looked through Mum's change, searching for a Canberra Two Bob and we collected them. I kept mine in a bunny eggcup that sat on the top shelf of the kitchen dresser. Yes, I had about six of them right up to adulthood when I passed them on to one of my daughters, who collects coins.

In comparing the 1930s with present times, one of the most striking differences that I remember was the attitude to pets, particularly dogs. When I go for a walk now, every second person I see is walking a dog. They are groomed, well fed and most are allowed inside the house. In the 1930s, a dog's place was out in the yard, chained to a kennel and never allowed inside the house. None of my relations or my school friends had a dog. Attitudes have changed over the years.

Another early memory of the 1930s is going to the dentist. We went to Mr Hughes in Beaumont Street, in Hamilton. The surgery was in an ordinary grey weatherboard house with a verandah and bay window. It was the only house in Beaumont Street; the other buildings were shops. The dentist chair was in a front room that used to be a bedroom. I thought that Mr Hughes was an old man and his dental nurse was his old wife. They both wore white coats and he had a foot pedal drill. I'm not kidding! His dentist drill was operated with his feet. He sat on a high seat and pedalled this machine to drill teeth. This was 1932 when I was five.

I have often asked myself the question: Why did I have a filling on a first tooth when we cleaned our teeth every day? The answer is probably because we cleaned our teeth first thing in the morning before breakfast and never before going to bed. We did not know then that it was important to clean teeth after the last meal of the day. It seems so logical today but the public had to be educated. That came later.

I can also remember on another occasion having an extraction. I was scared stiff, but I was given the tooth to take home. I put it in a glass of water overnight and in the morning the Tooth Fairy had left thrippence, which went straight into the moneybox. Incidentally, the little silver coin worth three pence was always called 'thrippence' by Australians. The correct word was thruppence, but this sounded too English for us so we called it 'thrippence'.

The cost of the extraction was two shillings and six pence. I remember that my dad bought me a thrippenny ice-cream after the visit to the dentist. It was my first thrippenny ice-cream and was much bigger than the kids' penny ice-cream with a pink cone. It had a light brown cone and was three times the size.

Mowing the lawn in the 1930s was very different to today's motorised mowers. We had a mower that was manually pushed back and forth, and the rotation of the wheels drove the blades.

Chapter 1 My Earliest Memories

Before they were available commercially, Dad made a homemade grass catcher with galvanised iron and hessian, which he fitted behind the mower to catch the grass.

Other memories include Christmases and birthdays. Our family always celebrated birthdays with a family party and the birthday cake was always a decorated sponge with a collar. The collar was decorative coloured paper, which was pinned around the cake. The candles were lit and blown out in the traditional manner.

On my fifth birthday, my cousins Jack and Joyce Attwood, as well as my aunties Eva, Nell and Jean, came to Queens Road. Joyce and I were close in age and we were being very 'naughty' by ringing the front door bell then quickly running around the back. However, as we ran down the side concrete path beside the house, I tripped and fell. I remember it clearly. The concrete path seemed to come up and hit me, as if in slow motion. I can still see it approaching. My forehead hit the concrete with force because it was inclined downhill. I bawled my eyes out. Luckily there was no blood, but a lump that felt as big as half a boiled egg appeared on my forehead. I was ushered upstairs and received lots of hugs. Auntie Jean came to the rescue and rubbed butter on the huge lump. Butter was the cure for bumps and bruises in the 1930s; probably only psychological. I'll never forget my fifth birthday.

I was allowed one friend for my sixth birthday, and those that followed. My schoolmate, Ken Wardell, came to all my birthday parties. My grandparents always gave me a two-shilling coin in an envelope for my birthday. For some reason, I didn't spend it but put the unopened envelope in the bottom of my dressing table drawer and kept several of them for years.

One year, Auntie Jean and Auntie Nell gave me an autograph book, which was about eight inches by three inches. In the early 1930s, collecting autographs from friends was fashionable. There weren't just signatures; friends usually wrote a verse of poetry or a wise saying. There were several on a page and some at odd angles. My aunties showed me their autograph books and they were crammed with little verses and sayings. I remember some were philosophical wise sayings, some were pleasant verses, and others were attempting to be funny. I guess it reflected the personality of the writer. One that was typical was, 'By hook or by crook, I'll be last in this book'. It was written on the back page, then someone else would write the same verse on the cover and the next person wrote the verse on the outside cover at an angle across the bottom right-hand corner.

Mum would occasionally look at her autograph book with fondness as she was reminded of friends. Collecting autographs from friends was popular in the 1930s. However, my autograph book only had my primary school teachers' signatures when I threw my book away.

At Christmas, we hung a sock for each child in front of the fireplace. In the morning it was filled with fruit, ginger and nuts. A big banana nearly filled a small sock, but the ginger was delicious. I can remember using Dad's hammer on the laundry step to crack open all the nuts on Christmas morning. There was always a toy.

Before Christmas, Mum made her own decorations. She bought a couple of streamers of different colours and cut them into short lengths then glued the ends together forming links in a chain. She never bought glue, she always mixed a little ordinary cooking flour with some water and made her own glue. Using drawing pins, Mum strung streamer chains from the central light to the corners of the kitchen, as well as draping them along the mantelshelf. After Christmas she would store them in a box to be used next year.

Mum always carefully saved Christmas paper wrappings to be used again next year. I remember her cursing Sellotape when it arrived in the late 1930s because it damaged the Christmas wrappings and they could not be used again. Christmas dinner was special with a roast dinner followed by Christmas pudding, and there were always a few sixpences in the pudding. Childhood memories of Christmases in the 1930s were happy memories in spite of the Depression.

Social habits varied greatly in the 1930s; for example, friends would visit spontaneously without a prior arrangement. With no mobile phones and few people owning telephones, I guess it was understandable, but friends just arrived and knocked on the door to visit someone. I can remember friends arriving and the excitement of the greeting with a happy, 'Come on in!' followed by, 'Let me take your coats to the bedroom'. It was the social custom to lay the visitors' winter coats on the main bedroom bed.

If there were babies or small children, they also were placed on the host's main bed if the visit was in the evening. There were no babysitters then; visitors took their children with them. So, a good housewife always had to have a tin of cakes or biscuits in the cupboard for supper for unexpected visitors. Times have changed. Sometimes when one of these unexpected visitors arrived in the afternoon and conversations extended until evening, the host felt obliged to say, 'Stay for tea', hoping that there was enough food in the cupboard. There usually was.

So, my earliest memories are happy memories, all centred around my family and the Tighes Hill house. It was my 'little world'; the sunny glassed-in verandah, the comfort of the warmth radiating from the fuel stove, the closeness of a family, and my pencils and watercolour paints filled my life with good memories.

CHAPTER 2
My Parents

My mother, Amy Frances Peacock, was born in a little country town called Watergumben in western New South Wales, between Cowra and Condobolin. It does not exist now. Her father was a country school teacher, so she told stories of growing up in government residences and moving from town to town every few years as school pupil numbers fluctuated. She had five sisters and one brother; my mother was the second eldest.

Besides being the local school teacher, her father was a Justice of the Peace. He was able to help country people with legal matters by signing papers, so he was highly respected.

My mother recalled that the family owned a horse and sulky and that gave them a certain social status in that era. They also had a cow. At that time, they had tank water and used candles and kerosene lamps at night in small country towns. After leaving school, Mum worked as a telephonist at the Hamilton Telephone Exchange before she was married. She sat with a row of young ladies facing a switchboard, wearing earphones with a curved speaker on her chest. She took telephone calls from the general public and connected the callers to the requested numbers by inserting a brass plug into the switchboard. This was the way a manual exchange operated in the late 1920s and early 1930s, years before automatic exchanges.

As soon as Mum announced that she was about to be married she had to resign from her employment, as married women were not allowed to work in the 1920s and 1930s.

As I have written previously, my mother handled money well. As soon as she and my father were engaged, they bought a block of land for two hundred pounds at Tighes Hill, a suburb of Newcastle, as my father was working there at that time, and they made arrangements for a house to be built. My mother said that she was determined not to pay rent, and for the whole of her life she never did.

My father, John Daniel Revel Grimmond, was born in 1901 in Minmi, a coal-mining town west of Newcastle. His father, also John Daniel Revel Grimmond, was a coal miner working for John Brown, who owned the Minmi coal mine. John Brown owned the houses in which his workers lived, as well as the railway line to Hexham. He was a very wealthy man.

Dad's father volunteered to fight in the Boer War in

South Africa. Dad was born after his father came home from the war. My grandfather returned to his work in the Minmi coal mine but he would often just lean his pick against the mine wall, walk outside, sit under a tree and cry uncontrollably when he thought of the war. He suffered from Post-Traumatic Stress Disorder (PTSD) resulting from his wartime experiences, but they did not know about PTSD in those days, so he was confined to a mental hospital for the rest of his life. As a result, Dad had no father growing up. John Brown allowed Dad's mother to live in a company house at Minmi until the family was old enough to work. Dad's mum 'took in' washing and Dad delivered milk on horseback as a young boy. He told me how he rode a horse, leaned over to reach the taps on the milk tanks, and filled the housewives' jugs when he called out, 'Milko!' It must have been a hard life for the family.

Dad left school as early as possible and began his working life as a telegram boy at Carrington, a suburb of Newcastle. 'What was a telegram boy?' I hear you ask. In those days, when someone wanted to contact another person quickly, they sent a  telegram. To do this, they filled in a form at a post office using the minimum of words, because it was one shilling for twelve words. The post office telegraphed the message by Morse Code to the post office nearest the recipient, where it was typed onto a form called a telegram and delivered by a boy on a bike to the person to whom it was addressed.

Dad told an interesting story of when he was a telegram boy at Carrington Post Office in his early teens. He was asked to deliver a telegram to the *Endurance,* a huge sailing ship that was tied up at Carrington wharf. The captain, Ernest Shackleton, after reading the telegram, said that he was about to change position to another wharf and asked Dad if he would like to steer the ship. Naturally he was excited, and rushed to carry his bike up the gangplank and rest it alongside the ship's rail. Then, under Ernest Shackleton's guidance, he steered the now famous *Endurance* to another wharf in Newcastle Harbour. The *Endurance* had a coal-fired steam engine, as well as sail, and probably used steam in the harbour. Dad occasionally mentioned in conversation that he steered the famous polar explorer's ship from one wharf to another in Newcastle Harbour. He was so proud of this story.

After many years as a telegram boy, Dad became a postman and delivered letters all over Carrington. In the 1930s, the postman walked from house to house carrying a large leather bag full of letters. He blew a whistle when he placed a letter in the letterbox to let the residents know that they had mail. The sound of the whistle let everyone know that the postman was coming closer to their house. There were two mail deliveries each weekday, one in the morning and one in the afternoon, as well as a Saturday morning delivery. Dad later worked at the Newcastle Post Office sending telegrams. That is how he met my mother at the Hamilton Telephone Exchange.

Chapter 2 My Parents

At the time my parents were engaged to be married, Dad was working for Jack Crocket at the plaster works at Tighes Hill, both making and installing sheet fibrous-plaster. I can only assume that he left the post office for better pay. That is why they bought a block of land at Tighes Hill, to be near his work. Mum tells the story that when Dad's boss, Jack Crocket, asked them, 'When are you two going to get married?', she cheekily replied, 'When you give us our plaster ceilings and walls for a wedding present.'

The response was that he offered to give them free plaster for their new house. Not only did he supply all the plaster, he also gave them highly decorative ceilings with wreaths of flowers cast in plaster for all four rooms including the kitchen and second bedroom, which was most unusual for the times and a curiosity for future owners.

Mum and Dad were married in April 1926 and went to Katoomba for their honeymoon. They moved into the completed house on their return. My mother was a good organiser.

You might ask: How could they afford a five-hundred-pound house so young? Apparently, my mother borrowed five hundred pounds, interest free, from her father. She paid it back at a pound a week – fifty-two pounds a year for ten years. My grandfather gave Mum an electric kettle as a present in 1936, for never missing a payment.

Mum posted the *Newcastle Herald* to my grandfather on a Friday. She only sent the centre pages for the week because in those days the *Newcastle Herald* had classified advertisements on the front page, and headlines were in the middle of the paper. She had a clever way of rolling it up. She folded it lengthwise then folded it inwards and tied a string through the two loops before wrapping it in the one-penny postal wrapper. I used to colour in pictures in the paper for Grandpa, mainly the furniture advertisements, so my brown pencil was always short from being used a lot. I rode my three-wheeler bike to the post box on the corner of John Street and William Street. Looking back, I think that may have contained a one-pound bank note sent to her father for a penny.

Dad continued working at Crockett's Plaster works until I was born in July 1927, when my mother said that with the responsibilities of parenthood he needed a more secure job, so Mum suggested that he get a government job. Dad joined the New South Wales Government Railways in 1927, and worked at the Honeysuckle Point Railway Workshop, which was between the Newcastle Harbour wharves and Hunter Street in the centre of Newcastle. He was only there a short while when the Depression struck and he was given the alternative of being 'stood down' or go 'on the track'.

He chose to go on the track, which meant that he camped on the job and laid railway lines in north-western New South Wales for many years. I can remember the long walk to Hamilton or Waratah Railway Station with my mother carrying a kerosene tin by a wire handle. It contained my father's food for a week; porridge, flour, bacon and eggs. It was addressed to where he was at the time and put on a train.

I also remember long winter nights in front of the fuel fire with Dad away.

Years later, he often recalled the hard work he did on the track. All the ballast, or rock base, was laid by hand with wheelbarrows, then the sleepers were manually laid. The long length of railway line was carried by two rows of men with heavy tongs and fixed in position with 'dog spikes' using large hammers. Dog spikes were forged pins with large heads. The holes in the sleepers for the dog spikes were drilled manually with two men standing and using a hand drill. It was very labour-intensive hard work, but it provided employment and extended the railway network further west.

Dad often brought something home from the northwest. One time he brought home a dingo pup, but it cried during the night and the neighbours complained. The police shot the pup because we were not allowed to have a pet dingo at that time.

Another time Dad brought home a tortoise. He drilled a hole on the edge of its shell and tethered it with a string near a dish of water. I had it for a while but one morning it was gone; the string had broken.

The most successful pet he brought home was a pink and grey galah. It made a lot of noise but became a good family pet. When we went on holidays, we left it with Uncle George and his family. They taught it to talk and they liked it so much that they wanted to keep it, so they did.

Because Dad spent so much time working in the northwest, I became familiar with the names of the places he was continually mentioning and knew the names of Narrabri,

Boggabri, Gunnedah, Willow Tree, Murrurundi, Aberdeen, Scone, Werris Creek and Muswellbrook at a very young age.

Finally, the track work ended and Dad came back to Honeysuckle Workshops where he did a course for operating a steam boiler. After gaining his certificates he was sent to Stony Creek, between Wauchope and Taree, where a rail bridge was being constructed over Stony Creek. Rather than camp, Mum rented a disused farm hut nearby. Mum and I and another railway family moved into the hut to look after the husbands.

I remember it well. I would have been four years old. One day while Mum was boiling milk in the stone fireplace, a large brown snake must have smelled it, and came up the back steps and into the hut. Mum lifted me up onto the table while the other wife ran for the men. I can still remember this. I also remember shots being fired from the .22 rifle, but the snake slithered under the hut after a great deal of anxiety and concern.

Dad was operating the steam boiler and pump, which was pumping water out of big steel cylinders standing in the creek where the bridge pylons were going. Each cylinder was about six feet in diameter and about twenty feet high. When they were empty of water, the concrete pylon was constructed inside it.

One day, I carried a lump of coal from the heap to the boiler in my small pink and blue wooden wheelbarrow that my mother had brought from home. Dad put the lump of coal in the fire door of his boiler.

I remember standing alongside the railway line with a line of men when a train was going past. We cupped our hands to our mouths and called out, 'Paper! Paper!'

Newspapers came fluttering out of the train windows and the men quickly picked them up. This was normal in those days, when there were no radios to keep up with the news. I often drive past Stony Creek and remember staying in the little hut, although there is a modern house in the same place these days.

Dad passed more exams and was eventually in charge of the main boiler, sending steam all around the Honeysuckle Railway Workshops. Gradually steam power was replaced by individual electric motors and the boilers were removed. His next job was operating the 'coffee pot'. This was the affectionate name given to the mobile steam crane. Dad had to both fire the boiler to keep the steam up and operate the tall jib crane. It was mainly used to charge the cast-iron furnace as well as unload trucks in the yard.

Dad with workmates at the Honeysuckle Workshops in front of the 'coffee pot' crane

Dad progressed to a machine moulder. In the late 1930s, Sydney had very fast electric trains that needed hard braking to stop in the length of a station. This meant that the soft cast-iron brake shoes would not last long and had to be replaced regularly, making it necessary to produce them at the same rate. The brake shoes were made at Newcastle in the Honeysuckle cast-iron foundry. Firstly, the aluminium pattern was pressed into moulding sand in a machine, hence the name machine moulding. The pattern was removed then two boxes placed on top of each other. Runners and risers dug into the sand and the cast-iron was poured into the mould, which was cooled and dressed then sent to Sydney for the electric trains.

Dad was tall – six foot two inches and proud of it. I have included a photograph taken on my quarter plate camera at the Islington house.

I remember every second Thursday Dad removing his pay envelope from his shirt pocket at tea time, opening it with a dinner knife and tipping the contents onto the tablecloth. He handed all the notes to Mum, a five-pound note and two one-pound notes, gathered up a few silver coins for himself and placed them in a leather purse. He did this for years and years, although probably in later years his pay came by cheque.

Two things stick in my memory about my father; one was rolling a cigarette and the other was shaving. It was a ritual on both occasions. He smoked Log-Cabin Fine Cut Tobacco that came in a neat little rectangular tin with a hinged lid. Firstly, he would remove a single sheet of cigarette paper from its little cardboard container and hold it by one corner between his lips. After doing this he *always* had to comment about something and spoke from the side of his mouth with his lips pressed together holding the cigarette paper.

Dad, John (Jack) Grimmond

Next, he opened the tin and dug out a quantity of tobacco with thumb and forefinger and placed it in the cupped palm of his left hand. The tin was closed and replaced in his pocket and he rubbed his two palms together, slowly and firmly.

He removed the cigarette paper from his lips and placed it on top of the small brown heap of tobacco. The next action was a dramatic flourish with a sweeping movement that reversed the cigarette paper from above the tobacco to beneath the tobacco. Supple fingers evenly spread the tobacco the full length of the paper, then he delicately commenced rolling with his thumbs until the edge with glue was visible the full length of the cigarette. He held it in one hand and licked its full length along the edge with the tip of a moist tongue, and pressed down firmly. Any protrusions of tobacco at each end were plucked out and let fall on the floor. After another close examination the cigarette was placed in the corner of his mouth with lips rounded inwards, then the pocket slapping started to find the matches. A wax match was removed from the little cylindrical box, and although it could be easily struck on the sandpaper bottom, Dad sometimes showed off by striking it on the seat of his trousers. Quick friction on any surface would ignite the blue-headed wax match. For this reason, these matches were eventually banned and replaced by wooden matches in rectangular boxes. With the match blazing, Dad skilfully wiped the end of the cigarette with the burning match to deposit some melting wax on the end of the cigarette. After the end was lit, there were dramatic withdrawals and puffs of air to cause the end to glow, followed by the expulsion of the first lungful of smoke, and a satisfied sigh. Dad rolled his own cigarettes most of his life, only giving up smoking when he retired.

Speaking of my father's habits, he never had an alcoholic drink in his life. Also, he never bet on a horse race. It was probably because of his Methodist background.

The second ritual that intrigued and amused me as a kid was his performance of weekend shaving. It could take an hour! I remember another family friend on a farm who also took over an hour for the weekend shave, so Dad was not unique. It began by chopping a few lighting sticks, as in the summer the kitchen fire would have gone out by the afternoon. With the fire revived and the kettle on the stove, he hunted around for his shaving gear. A large shaving mug, a brush, a cut-throat razor, a leather strop, a mirror and two towels were found in the bathroom.

Inside the shaving mug were always several small pieces of soap. We never threw out the end of a cake of soap, the last little bit was put into Dad's shaving mug, so there was always a collection of thin pieces of well-used bits of soap inside the mug. Dad poured boiling water from the kettle over the soap, at  the same time beating furiously with the brush to make a mug full of thick foam. One towel was spread out on the kitchen table and another was draped across his shoulders covering his chest. He rolled his shirt collar inwards around his neck. The mirror was removed from the bathroom and leaned against the flour canister, which was placed on the kitchen table.

Next came the all-important razor stropping. The leather strop was hooked onto a doorknob or the back of a chair and the leather handle was held firmly in the left hand, pulling the strop at about forty-five degrees to the vertical. While holding the opened razor by the white handle in his right hand, he pulled the sharp blade carefully along the strop. With a quick flip over, the razor was then drawn back in the opposite direction. This continued for about ten to fifteen minutes with a very serious expression of concentration on the face. Without fail, he always tested its sharpness by scraping it along a few hairs on his left forearm, creating a little bare patch. As a kid, I was amused at the bare patch on a hairy arm.

Then came the serious business. Sitting with his legs spread out, Dad reached for the mug and applied a generous Santa Claus beard of dazzling white foam all over his face, with only his eyes and nose visible above it. He checked in the mirror. Then, pulling a face with a most unusual expression, chin extended, eyebrows raised, mouth slightly open and eyes looking down his nose at the mirror, came the first tentative scrape. When seemingly satisfied with the result, the process began in earnest and vast areas of bare skin replaced the white foamy beard. With the razor filled with white foam and speckled with black whiskers, it was carefully wiped clean on a tissue. Then the other side was commenced. I don't know why, but at this stage in the procedure he always seemed to be talking about something and needed to gesticulate with the open razor being waved in the air as if to make a point. It happened every time.

When it came to shaving the upper lip, there seemed to

be a special ritual. For some unknown reason, he always held the tip of his nose with the thumb and forefinger of his left hand. Whether it was to hold the head still or stretch the skin, I have no idea. It may have been to give the left hand something to do, but he always held his nose steady while he shaved the upper lip. Again, the razor was wiped clean and then the throat was next. With chin stretched as high as possible and lips pressed tightly together, he would start the delicate job of shaving around his Adam's Apple, as well as the rest of the throat. I remember watching most anxiously, as I believed that one slip meant certain death, and gave a sigh of relief when it was safely completed. With a final cleaning of the razor on the tissue, tensions were relaxed as the face was vigorously rubbed with the towel, at the same time turning left and right, and patting the face while looking in the mirror.

At this stage he examined his face for little cuts from the sharp razor. Inevitably, there would be one or two very small nicks that were starting to show bleeding spots on his face. This called for cigarette paper. A single paper was withdrawn from the packet and carefully torn into four square pieces that were placed on the bleeding cuts. They were held in place by the wet blood. I thought it looked extremely funny. Apparently, years later, Norman Gunston thought so too. Pieces of cigarette paper stuck to his face with drops of blood in the centre was a 'trade mark' for Garry McDonald's comedy acts.

Dad's collar was finally turned outwards, and the job was complete. I have never used a cut-throat razor in my life.

Perhaps it's because of those memories. My brother and I, both in our nineties, still chuckle when we recall our dad shaving in the 1930s.

Another memory of Dad's unusual habits was of him cutting his toenails. He used a pocketknife. When they had grown long, he reached up on top of the dresser where he kept his sharp pocketknife safely away from children, and proceeded to pare the toenails down very carefully one by one with a unique skill that fascinated two young boys at the time.

There were a few differences in men's clothes between then and now. Firstly, men wore a waistcoat with a suit in the 1930s. This was a sleeveless jacket with a row of buttons down the front and, would you believe, it was not polite to do them all up; the bottom one was always left undone. In the early 1900s, King Edward VII was too fat to do up the last button so everyone at the function he was attending undid their own bottom button, so that the king would not feel uncomfortable; and since then, the custom has continued. So, for this reason alone, men do not do up the last button of a waistcoat.

Most men held their watch in their waistcoat pocket with a chain; usually gold, draped in two loops from side to side. Any medals they owned could be attached to the chain. Dad always wore his Railway Ambulance medals, especially his Gold Life medal, on his watch chain.

Most men wore armbands. These had spring-loaded links that expanded when putting them on, and then they contracted into position. Their purpose was to pull the cuffs firmly into the wrists.

Men also wore sock suspenders. These were elastic garter-type bands worn around their calves, with a press-stud that gripped the sock to stop the socks from slipping down.

Cuff links were common, as were collar studs, and all dress shirts had detachable collars.

Ties were tied in the old 'four-in-hand' knot long before the modern Windsor knot. Men always wore a black bow tie with a dress suit. Tiepins were common for long ties.

All men wore hats and they took them off indoors. There was a ritual with hats; men always raised their hats when they greeted a lady, even when walking along the street, as if to say 'Good morning' and show respect. Of course, they did not raise their hats when greeting another man.

Men always placed a black band around their hats when they went to a funeral, and they wore a black armband as well. If men were in the street when a funeral passed by, they stood still, removed their hats and bowed their heads, even if they did not know the person being buried. Incidentally, funerals were fairly common, and the procession of cars always drove slowly behind the hearse with their lights on. Other traffic would pull over and stop.

Another men's fashion in the 1930s were braces. These were elastic straps worn over the shoulders to hold trousers up. Even little kids wore braces. They were attached to the trousers by

Dad's watch and ambulance medals

two buttons at the back and two buttons on each side at the front. I could be insensitive to mention this, but going to the toilet was quite a feat if a man was wearing a jumper or cardigan over his braces. They had to undo the back two buttons and allow the ends of the braces to be pulled up behind the neck to enable the pants to be pulled down. To reach the braces and do them up again was a physical challenge.

It was not polite for the braces to be seen in public, so anyone who got into a tram without a coat with his braces showing received glances of disapproval from all the passengers. It was just not done.

Another item of clothing worn by men in the 1930s was a pair of knickerbockers. These were long trousers that buttoned at the cuffs, holding the trousers firmly around the ankles. Uncle Jack, Mum's younger brother, wore them. I remember putting on a pair of knickerbockers that someone must have given us, and saying to my mother, 'I feel funny. They look ridiculous. Please cut them off at the knees and make shorts.' Which she did. As a fashion, I don't think they lasted very long.

Women's fashions are always changing, but in general, women's dresses were longer in the 1930s. Under their dresses, women wore corsets. These were stiffened panels that were laced tightly around the waist. Mum wore these for years. I also remember Mum having a 'fur'. This was a fox fur with a fox head and glass eyes. It even had little feet and a long bushy tail. Women wore furs around their necks, either for warmth or fashion. It fascinated me as a small child, and I used to pat it.

Women's clothes and shoes often had buttons so most women had a range of buttonhooks. These were small hooks of various sizes, usually with decorative handles, that hooked a button and threaded it through a loop or buttonhole.

After Mum had paid off the Tighes Hill house, we moved into another house on Maitland Road in Islington. The second house was 'spec built'; that is, a builder purchased a block of land, built a house to his own design and put it on the market as a speculation. The house and land cost

850 pounds in 1936. It was at 26 Maitland Road, Islington, which is actually on the Pacific Highway. The road was always busy with traffic but the house was convenient to the shops in Hamilton and I could still walk to Tighes Hill School.

Mum put a tenant in the Tighes Hill house and she paid off the loan on the Islington house with the rent from the Tighes Hill house. Looking back now, I admire my mother's financial skills.

One of my memories of living in the Islington house was going to the Railway picnics. Trade Unions were very strong in the 1930s and they negotiated a 'Picnic Day' in their employment agreements. One day a year, employees of a particular trade or industry were paid to have a day's holiday so they could all go for a picnic with fellow employees and their families. There was a day for the Butchers' Picnic, the Bakers' Picnic, the Railway Workers' Picnic, and so on. Not all unions organised an actual picnic; some took a day's pay in-lieu, but it was traditional that all the workers from the Honeysuckle Railways Workshops had a family picnic.

The Newcastle Railway Picnic was always held at Blackalls Park. Blackalls is a Newcastle suburb near Toronto on Lake Macquarie and, of course, accessible by train. The picnic train went from Newcastle Station, when it was at the head of Hunter Street, and picked up picnickers along the way, who held long red ribbons out of the train windows and waved to everyone. The driver blew the whistle almost continually. Everyone was in a happy, festive mood. Over a thousand people walked from Blackalls Station to the park, then spread around the area in family groups. The first events were the children's age races, followed by the egg-and-spoon race, where runners ran holding a hard-boiled egg on a dessert spoon at arm's length, and then the sack race, where the runners were waist deep in a chaff bag. There were also three-legged races and wheelbarrow races. In the three-legged race, a couple had two legs tied together with a handkerchief, and in the wheelbarrow race, a person's legs were held under a second person's arms and the runner literally ran on his hands. Throughout the day there were broom-throwing contests for the ladies, and Wellington-boot-throwing contests for the men. Steel quoits were always popular, as well as tug-of-war battles for teams of men.

There were announcements over the loudspeaker seemingly all the time, telling people where the next event was taking place. The committee hired rowing boats and there were rowing races with singles and pairs. Dad always did well in those races because of his long arms. There were stalls and chocolate wheels run commercially by outsiders. I remember a team of performers who rode motorbikes around vertical walls in a cylindrical enclosure. The noise went on all day. There were always free bags of lollies for the kids, as well as pieces of fruit. Hot water was free, and there was a steady stream of fathers with teapots at lunchtime. Some kids took their bathing suits and swam in Blackalls baths. This was a rectangular enclosure of vertical tea-tree posts in the lake, with a diving board in one corner.

There was always a happy atmosphere at Railway picnics and they were fun days. Friends met and talked for ages. I was proud of my good attendance at school but I made an exception for Picnic Day and took a day off.

I mentioned before that unionism was strong in Newcastle in the 1930s, and so was support for Labour Day, or May Day, as the locals referred to it. The first Monday in May was always a public holiday, but the Newcastle people made it a 'workers' day' by supporting a procession of all the unions in a march down Hunter Street to Number 1 Sports Ground at Cooks Hill. Dad always attended the march and walked behind the banner of the ARU (Australia Railways Union). The floats depicted poor working-class men demanding higher wages from their rich employers. Newcastle people lined the streets and cheered them on. The procession ended at the sports ground where entertainment took place. Children wearing colourful costumes danced the Maypole dance with ribbons streaming from the top of the pole; there were also girls performing Scottish dances over crossed swords. One year, the police union had two motorbikes, each drawing a Roman chariot; the drivers, dressed in Roman clothes, operated the two police bikes standing in the chariots. A pair of these raced around the oval. It was most spectacular. Of course, there were speeches from Labor MPs; in general, it was a happy atmosphere.

I remember that there were large photographs of Joseph Stalin in the May Day procession. He was a hero of the working class; so much so that the Railway Union raised money and sent a member to Russia to be a guest of their government and observe Stalin's Five-Year Plan. When the member returned, he gave lectures to trade unions in Australia. The person selected was Arthur Outridge from the Honeysuckle Workshops. He was a good friend of Dad's. When Arthur returned, he gave lectures to union members explaining Stalin's Five-Year Plans. At that time, Stalin said that Russia was ten years behind the leading countries of the world and Russia had to catch up. So he was building massive dams, generating power and constructing factories. He introduced collective farming where 'the people' owned the farms not individuals. Bread was free, so there was no hunger or poverty. It was a planned economy with a socialist government. Russia was the envy of the world through working-class eyes in the 1930s, but somehow the socialists turned into communists, and Russia became a dictatorship with a minority ruling party. Things changed and communism became the enemy of the capitalist countries (at least that is how I saw it as a kid).

Dad remained 'in the Railway' until retirement. My parents enjoyed a long retirement at their Islington home, then they moved to Port Macquarie to St Agnes Retirement Village in 1987 to be near me. My father and mother both died in 1990, at age eighty-eight and eighty-seven respectively.

CHAPTER 3

The Great Depression

My memories of the Great Depression are very vivid. Even as a preschool child, I was very aware that people were out of work and begging for money to live. The official figure was almost 32% unemployment in New South Wales in mid-1932, but it seemed much more in the Newcastle suburbs. We had several callers every day. They would offer to dig the garden or chop wood or just asked for 'a few bob, please lady, to feed m' family'. Mum never gave them money but she always gave them a cup of tea on the back steps.

Then came the singers and musicians. They would stand on the street corner and sing at the top of their lungs or play a mouth organ, and sometimes a violin or concertina was played most vigorously; then they would take around an upturned hat from door to door asking for coins. The ones I liked the best were the bell ringers. They had a collapsible table and a row of little bells, descending in size. They could produce wonderful tunes but their only audience was a row of half-a-dozen Queens Road pre-schoolers sitting along the kerb.

Then there were the door-to-door salesmen, those men

who took the initiative to sell something. My favourite was the blackberry man. He picked a kerosene tin full of ripe, juicy blackberries and carried the tin with a wire handle from door to door, selling the blackberries for thrippence a cupful. They smelled delicious. My mum always bought some and we would have a blackberry pie.

There was also a man going from door to door selling freshly picked gum-tips. These, as the name suggests, were bunches of the little reddish leaves of the new growth of gum leaves. In the 1930s it was popular to have gum-tips displayed in a flower vase; something you would never see these days. Mum never spent money on them, but whenever we went for a picnic in the bush, she always brought home a bunch of gum-tips to place in one or two vases to decorate the house. They also provided a pleasant eucalyptus smell.

Then came the Rawleigh's man. He carried a heavy suitcase from door to door loaded with ointments and cures for ailments, like a walking chemist shop. He was always popular. Rawleigh's ointment was used in most households for cuts, scratches and bruises.

Next was the 'clothes props' man. He went into the bush and cut down small saplings with forked ends. These were used to hold up the backyard clothesline that went from fence to fence. We had swivel arms with two lines and did not need a prop, but most people had a single line held up with bush clothes props that often broke when kids rode them like horses. These clothes props were about nine feet long so he carried them with a horse and cart. The cart was often overloaded and they almost touched the ground at the back. He drove the horse very slowly and gave a mournful cry of 'Clothes props!' to announce his wares.

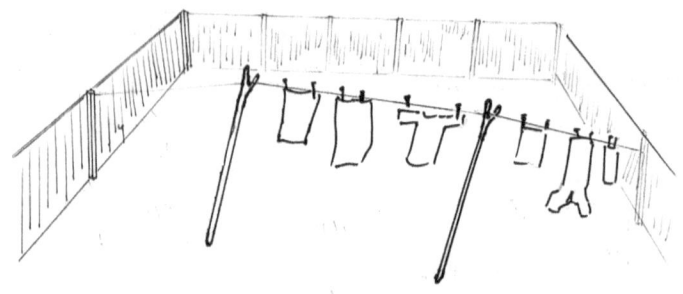

Also arriving by horse and cart was the 'bottle-oh' man. He also drove his horse and cart slowly and called out, 'Bottle-oh!', in a loud voice that had the children running for a few pennies for their empty bottles.

And to add to the sights and sounds of Depression days, we also had the 'Rabbit-oh' man. He shot or trapped rabbits, cleaned and skinned them, and had them in the bottom of his cart covered with wet corn bags and a few blocks of ice. He sold them for ten pence a pair. The housewife would hear him coming when he called out, 'Rabbit-oh!' and they would rush out with a dinner plate.

So, with all this activity there was frequent noise and excitement on the suburban streets. Besides these occasional vendors there were the regular callers, also by horse and cart. Earliest in the morning was the milkman. His cart had built-in milk tanks with taps protruding from the back. He would jump down from his high seat, run around the back, and fill either a pint or a quart galvanised dipper by turning a handle at the back. Then he would run, holding the container level and empty it into the customer's jug. We left the money out on the front step in those days. It was thrippence halfpenny a pint and seven pence a quart. Sometimes our milkman would yodel to let customers know he was coming. Apparently, it was a tradition for milkmen to do that in those days.

There was also the baker. He came daily and carried his bread in a big basket over his arm. He went right to the back door, calling, 'Baker!' His basket was protected with a canvas cover that he would flip back as he handed the housewife the loaf or half-loaf, white or brown. Mum paid him with aluminium tokens that she had previously paid for at the Co-Op. He was always cheery and had a pleasant word for the customers.

Next was the greengrocer, who was Chinese. He had a huge draft horse and a very high cart. The housewives would gather around his cart, purchase their green groceries then carry them back to the house in their aprons, held outwards by the bottom corners to form a bowl. We kids were frightened of 'the Chinaman'; we never spoke to him but we were fascinated by his horse. Its feet were huge!

The caller who was always in a hurry was the coal man. He had a flat-top lorry loaded with bags of coal, all standing up. He wore a singlet and was always black with coal dust over his arms, shoulders and face. He backed up to his lorry and bent over so he could carry his heavy load on his back. He would run around the back and tip it into the coal heap and take his empty bag back to the truck.

I remember my mother's snow-white hand passing over six shillings into his blackened hand.

With all these horse-drawn carts, at the end of the day there were little brown heaps of horse manure dotted along Queens Road, so I would collect the coal shovel from the coal-box and push my billy-cart along the road and scrape up the horse manure for Dad's sweet pea garden. I 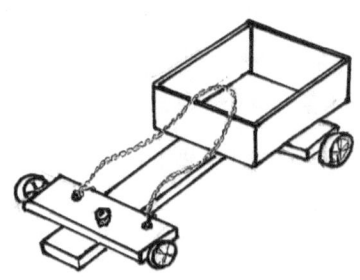 can't imagine modern-day kids doing that today. There was no need to dodge the traffic, there was none.

Also, there were 'swaggies'. Swaggies were men who walked from town to town with a blanket roll across their shoulders looking for work. We would see them everywhere, along the roads, in parks, around the beaches. They were depressed souls who just kept on walking, begging for food and sleeping anywhere. I felt sorry for swaggies.

Then, there was another sad side of the Depression. It was when families could not pay their rent and they were literally 'kicked out into the streets'. This led them to build temporary accommodation on vacant land. They seemed to collect in groups, which we called 'unemployment camps' (also called shanty towns), sometimes with hundreds of families in them.

There were several throughout Newcastle, including a big one at Carrington, one on the beach near Nobbies, one near the gas works in Steel Street, as well as several large camps at Wallsend. These were groups of temporary dwellings made of galvanised iron, old boxes, flattened kerosene tins, corn bags, fibro, even cardboard boxes. They were just humpies.

I must tell you a personal story. A few years ago, pre-Covid, my wife and I were on a tour of Brazil, South America, when the guide took us to the 'slums' for our supposed enlightenment. When our fellow tourists, mainly Australians, were disgusted at the poverty and the way people were living in humpies made of scrap materials, I was able to tell them that I witnessed the same conditions in Newcastle during the Depression of the 1930s.

When I turned five and was at school, I can remember the principal going from room to room asking, 'How many fathers are out of work?' and seeing more than half the class put up their hands. I remember clearly that when anyone ate an apple, there was a queue of kids asking if they could eat the core. They never had fruit. Sad memories.

The way the Depression affected my family was not having a father around for several years when he worked away from home laying railway lines. Fortunately, Dad was employed continually, but most of my school friends' dads were out of work.

Even though my family had a regular income, the atmosphere of the Depression was always there. *Everyone* was economical with spending; it generated an atmosphere of mental depression. Everyone was worried about the seriousness of the situation. People would walk an extra section to save a penny tram fare. Cousins and neighbours accepted 'hand-me-down' clothes from the older children, and clothes were patched, especially the seats of boys' pants. My mother, and I am sure many other mothers, saved every bit of string and brown paper to use again. Jam jars were kept and used over and over again. Nothing was wasted. Besides saving string and brown paper, every housewife had a button jar containing hundreds of buttons. No garment was thrown away with buttons still on it. They were removed and the cotton picked from the little holes. These were saved in a jar in case a button was needed to replace one on a shirt or a pair of trousers at a later date.

My mum would never allow two lights to be on at the same time; we all had to be in the same room at night. Even the teapot was completely 'drained' every time. Nothing was thrown out. Mum bought flour from the Co-Op in little linen bags with a blue CWS printed on them, standing for Co-Operative Wholesale Society. She unpicked the sewn edge and my brother and I used them for handkerchiefs right up to teenagers. We tried to cover up the printed letters as we used them.

As young kids we soon learnt that butter was a very expensive item and had to be used very sparingly. We were trained early to spread butter very thinly on bread, and reminded often that it was one shilling and eight pence a pound. I think Meadowlea, a substitute butter, was only seven pence halfpenny.

I guess bathing once a week, and clothes washing once a week, were cost-effective measures too. Mum was a master of economy. Years later, as an adult, I was discussing the Depression with my cousin, Jack Attwood, when he said, 'Our mothers did not know that the Depression was over.' It was true, that generation never changed, they were always very careful with money the whole of their lives. We changed 'school clothes' to 'house clothes' as soon as we came home so that one lot would do us for the week. And that was the way in every house, not just ours.

I can remember bringing home my straightened-out lunch

paper and brown paper bag so they could be used for the whole week. Economy was instilled into us until it became second nature. We were children of the Depression.

Another economical measure was cleaning our teeth with salt and baking soda. We always had a screw-top jar in the bathroom containing the mixture. I didn't use toothpaste until I was an adult. Only rich people used toilet paper in the 1930s. Most households used old newspapers. It was my job to use my school ruler as a straight edge and tear up newspaper into six-inch squares, make a hole in the corner with a skewer, tie them with a loop of string and hang them on a nail in the toilet. I am sure most families did the same.

When the sole of a shoe wore through, it could be repaired with a kit at home to save the expense of going to the bootmakers. Firstly, the worn sole was roughened up with a special piece of punched tin, then it was coated with a rubberised glue, allowed to stand for a while, then the new rubber sole was pressed into place with the handle of a claw hammer that rolled over the edges. The rubber sole was then trimmed with scissors or a knife while the shoe was on the last. A last was a cast-iron support for mending shoes. It had three feet shapes in three different sizes from large to small, and the shoe was fitted over the cast-iron sole pattern while it was worked on. Dad did all our shoe repairs on that last.

Homemade clothes were common. Mum bought a Singer sewing machine and made all my clothes, mainly from unpicked adult clothes. This was normal for the period. And children rarely went to the barbers. My father cut my brother's and my hair until we left home. The Depression era promoted initiative for a 'do it yourself' policy in home carpentry, house painting or cement laying. Women were always busy knitting socks and jumpers. I can remember my mother's 'fancy work'. This was embroidery needlework, mainly on tablecloths that involved hundreds of hours embroidering flowers and patterns of the most intricate designs. Dad always 'fixed' something that was broken, or patched it up some way to keep it working, so much so that we had a family expression that anything mended was called a 'Newcastle job'.

Dad's shed was like a museum, with collections of every size of nut, bolt, washer and screw, all second hand, that could be used again. He kept pieces of wire and tin, thinking that it could be used again somewhere. When Mum and Dad moved to their retirement home years later, there were many trips to the dump.

One of the unfortunate side-effects of the Depression was the crime rate. Not that it is an excuse, but people were desperate to survive and house robberies were common. Dad had his bike stolen from under our high house at Tighes Hill. He just leaned it against a pier near the toilet and one morning it was gone. He had to go to work by tram until he bought another second-hand one. The next one was kept in the laundry with the door locked each night.

We heard of people having furniture, clothes, and even in one case the entire household goods taken, including the lino. The neighbours thought the owners were moving out, but when they returned from a holiday the house was bare.

They were desperate times but the Depression created a certain breed of people who economised, 'made-do', and 'got-by' without spending much money, eventually surviving those difficult times.

The government created jobs in Newcastle by employing hundreds of men to make concrete roads through Adamstown, Broadmeadow, Merewether and Hamilton. It was labour-intensive work as men had to mix cement by hand and spread it using shovels and wheelbarrows, but the scheme worked. It was called Relief Work. Hundreds of men were employed. Newcastle had concrete roads with black tar expansion joints at regular intervals. These roads lasted for many years. It stimulated the economy and helped Newcastle through of the Depression.

CHAPTER 4

School

I remember very clearly going to Tighes Hill Primary School. It was a two-storey brick building with wide concrete steps at each end. My first day at school would have been late January in 1933. At that time, the kindergarten, first and second classes were both boys and girls, and occupied the lower level of the building. Upstairs were the girls' third to sixth classes, while the boys' third to sixth classes were in the old building next door. A paling fence separated the two playgrounds.

My first teacher was Miss Bakewell and she was assisted by Miss Connley. In retrospect, I think she may have been a student teacher, as it was odd to have two teachers. My early memories are of the two brown circles painted on the kindergarten room floor and playing 'drop the handkerchief' and running around a circle of boys and a circle of girls. We were told to take our shoes off. I suppose it was less noisy for the other classes.

Tighes Hill Kindergarten, 1933

At the end of the day there was a rush to put our shoes on, then there was a line-up for the teacher to tie the shoelaces. I remember the long line waiting to have laces tied so I hopped in and helped the teacher because I could tie bows. So, I became 'teacher's little helper' every time that happened.

Another memory of kindergarten was drawing on the little blackboards around the walls. After our morning story we had to draw the story on the boards and the best one was given coloured chalk to colour some part of the drawing. I can remember getting the coloured chalk most days. I could already draw.

When my parents asked me, 'How was school today?' I remember telling them that I had a girlfriend and her name was Lillian. I was only five years old. I always rushed to hold her hand when we were told to 'take a partner', and I always dropped the handkerchief behind her when we were playing 'drop the handkerchief'. I liked Lillian. One morning as I was leaving for school, I asked my mother if I could take Lillian a bunch of flowers from our garden. Mum had a pretty flower garden. Mum said, 'You can't take a bunch of flowers to school. The teachers would not put them in a vase of water for you and they would wilt before three o'clock. Take a small posy instead.'

So, she picked me a small spray, bound them with cotton thread and gave me a little gold safety pin. She showed me how to pin it on Lillian's dress. I proudly took it to school. I was holding it out in front of me when the teacher on playground duty put her hand out and said, 'Are those for me?'

I held them back and said, 'No. They are for Lillian!'

I soon found Lillian and pinned them on her dress. I wonder if she remembers it. I was friends with Lillian for all of my school years throughout the 1930s, but later in life we lost contact.

I remember my first Christmas tree. The kindergarten teacher asked the class if anyone's father could bring a tree to school. Leslie Griffith's father was a bottle-oh and had a horse and cart, so he delivered one to the school. I think it must have been the last day of school for the year when Leslie's father arrived with a small gum tree about three feet high. It was a rainy day and the little gum tree was dripping wet. I remember the trail of drips to the side of the kindergarten room and a frantic search for an empty garbage tin and a couple of bricks. Somehow, they found them and stood the dripping tree in the big garbage tin, held up with the bricks. It was too wet to decorate, so we sat in front of it and sang

Christmas carols. It looked a miserable little tree with a puddle of water around it. I felt sorry for it. However, that was my first Christmas tree.

On rainy days, there was always a congregation of mothers with overcoats and hats waiting at the school gate at three o'clock when the infants came out, especially if it had been a sunny morning.

I progressed to First Class the next year and had Miss Paul for a teacher. I remember reading my first story. It was 'The Cat Sat on the Mat' and the first story in the Red reader. We progressed from the Red reader to the Blue then the Brown reader. They gradually became more difficult to read. We only wrote with pencil in the government green-covered books, using lowercase printing between two blue lines in First Class and Second Class. At the end of the year, I remember coming first in the class in First Class for the boys and Joyce Webb came first for the girls. Miss Paul gave us each a penny for a prize. Of course, I put it straight in my moneybox with no thought of spending it.

Second Class was a change of room and we were the 'big people' of the Infants' school. I was Milk Monitor and had to stand by the crate of milk bottles in the playground at recess (we called it 'play-time') and cross off the pupils' names as I handed them their bottles of milk. Their parents paid five pence a week for them to have a penny bottle each day. My mother always gave me five pence for milk each week.

I was also Garden Boy with Bavin Evans. At three o'clock on Friday afternoon, the Garden Boys watered the school garden near the steps. We then rolled the hose up and put it away before 3.30 pm. We felt important being Garden Boys, but missed out on the Friday story.

It was while I was in Second Class, in 1935 aged eight, that I caught the measles. It was not unusual; I think every kid got it in turn around the class. The regulation time to stay at home was two weeks, which I did. I can remember staying in bed in my pyjamas all day, which was a new experience. My younger brother, Bruce, only three and not at school, would sit on my bed and talk to me during the day. Just as I was better and ready to return to school Bruce was covered in red spots, which meant that I had to have another two weeks at home because a student was not allowed to go to school if a sibling had measles.

Faced with having a month without schooling, my parents probably thought that I would fall behind in my school work, so they took me to stay with my cousins at Blackalls and I attended Toronto School for the regulation two weeks.

Uncle Cal and Mum's sister, Auntie Eva, ran a poultry farm. They had seemingly hundreds of laying fowls and sold eggs to the Egg Board in large square boxes. They also incubated their own chickens. All of this was fascinating to an eight-year-old, but the most unusual thing about living at Blackalls was walking to Toronto School *along the train line!*

Apparently the 'grown-ups' knew the timetables and considered it safe. I have distinct memories of jumping from sleeper to sleeper and sometimes doing a balancing act with arms spread out walking along the shiny steel railway line. My cousin and I were not the only ones; there were about half-a-dozen Blackalls kids attending Toronto School. It seemed like a couple of miles, but was probably less. We even had to cross a bridge over a creek. I did this every school day for two weeks. My cousin did it all her primary school life. It just wouldn't happen these days. It was only a branch line, but what if an unscheduled engine came along?

After the regulation two weeks was completed, I returned to Tighes Hill School, much relieved.

Third Class was a step up into the BIG school. I was aged eight going into Third Class in 1936, and I turned nine during the year. We had Mr Engert, a male teacher for the first time, and were in the old historic building, next door to the Infants.

It was straight into ink and 'running writing'. I remember the little white china inkwells in the middle of the desk for two people. We were given a wooden pen with a post office nib that was split down the middle to give thick down strokes and thin upstrokes. Our first exercise was 'butcher's hooks'. These were a sort of back-to-front straight 'S'. We did hundreds of them to get the feel of the thin upstroke, the thick downstroke, then the thin upstroke again. Every pupil held the pen exactly the same way, by thumb and middle finger, with the index finger straight and resting along the pen, and the pen pointing to the right shoulder. Incidentally, every pupil was right-handed except for one boy in our class. William Knight was the only left-handed boy in the school; that is, one in over one hundred, less than one per cent. In those days, parents insisted on giving children their first rattle and their first spoon in their right hand. I remember teachers coming from other rooms to watch William write because it was so unusual.

Then there was the all-important slope. We had slope cards behind our writing paper so we could see slope lines through the page, and we had to have all our butcher's hooks parallel and sloping forward about ten degrees from the vertical. The ink was wet so we had to avoid smudges, and blots fell from the nib. It was a lot for an eight-year-old all at one time. We had blotting paper and had to 'blot' or absorb excess ink to dry the writing.

Progressing from the butcher's hooks, we started to form our letters. The teacher hung a huge chart on the board with all the letters on it, both small and capital letters, and we copied them. It was then that I discovered that a capital Q was a big two. This fascinated me. We were being taught copperplate writing.

Learning to write with ink was a long hard battle. We were issued with free government green-covered books. They always had a 'new' smell. In Third Class, importance was placed on margins. The very first thing a pupil did when facing a new page was to draw a one-inch margin. This was always the width of our twelve-inch ruler that we had to purchase for one penny. They had centimetres and millimetres on the back which we regarded as a foreign language and never referred to them, but now it is the other way around.

The other thing that I remember about Third Class was Mr Engert's love for music. He had the whole school singing a two-part song called 'Waterlilies'. We would go over and join the girls to sing it in their assembly room upstairs. Mr Engert also offered to take pupils to the Newcastle Town Hall at night to hear the Vienna Boys' choir. It cost six shillings. Only six boys brought the money. Dad paid for me to go. He said I would never forget it, and obviously I never did. It was the best singing I had ever heard, with high, clear notes; it was wonderful.

From Third Class to Sixth Class, we received magazines every month. These were government-printed magazines for all New South Wales schools. They were foolscap with white glossy paper and about six to eight pages. We all had to purchase a strong cardboard magazine folder that would hold a year's supply, held in with a loop of string. Each month they contained a few stories, sometimes a poem and a few photographs. We read it aloud, in turns around the class. At the end of the year, we each had quite a thick bundle in our folder. We didn't take it home during the year, it remained under our desk ready for use.

Blackboards were different in the old school building. In First and Second Class our blackboards were flush with the wall because it was a new building. However, in the old building there were glass folding doors in front of the class rooms so blackboards were held on easels. These had large three-legged supports with a row of holes and round pegs for adjusting the height.

The teacher used white chalk and it was rubbed out with a chalkboard duster. This was a thick piece of blue felt attached to a wooden base. After a while it became so full of powdered chalk that it had to be cleaned. The method of

Chapter 4   School

Tighes Hill Fifth Class, 1938

Back Row: Reg Bradley, Stan Cotton, Merv Baker, Peter Tarrent, Merv Elsley, Don Christianson, **Richard Grimmond**, Max Shea, Allan Balks, Arthur Stewart

4th Row: Jackie Carr, Kerry Boyd, Les Evans, Jack Lonie, Roy Owens, Ken Wardell, Billy Lambert, Alex Frizell, Arthur Gibbons, Ken Woods

3rd Row: Alex McKenzie, Arthur Cole, Athol Armbrister, Frank Queenan, Ray Whitten, Bavin Evans, Ron Downie, Keith Dean, Neville Davies, Eddie Hunt,

2nd Row: Walter Berwick, William Winkworth, Billy Cox, Jim Beath, Stan Burton, Les Griffiths, Neville Princehorn, Max Valentine, Duan Phillips, Ray Young

Front Row: Billy Knight, Len Jordan, Rodney Drew, Bill Warby, 'Mick' Merv Jones, Max Matherson.

cleaning varied from teacher to teacher. Some hit two dusters against each other over the classroom bin. Others sent a boy outside to hit it on the step. Most of them, I called them the lazy ones, put their arm out of the window and hit it against the bricks below the window or on the sandstone windowsill, making very untidy marks outside the building that would stay there until the next rainy day.

Another memory of Third Class was playing marbles in the playground. There were games called big ring, little ring, and pothole. The playground was clay and gravel, ideal for drawing circles with a sharp stick. The controllers of the marble rings were the reverse order of the academic hierarchy in the classroom. They took control, drew the ring, decided who could play, and made sure everyone put the required number of marbles in the centre. It was always 'for keeps', which meant that if someone hit your marble out of the ring, he kept it. The serious marble players had cloth drawstring bags full of marbles that they had won. Big ring was played in a ring about a yard diameter and marbles were always fired from the edge of the ring. When playing little ring, about one foot diameter, the taw, or marble being fired, was fired from where it stopped rolling after the previous shot. Fortunes were won and lost among the good players. I am afraid I had no marble-firing ability and opted for pothole. This was played by digging a small hole about four inches diameter and three inches deep against a wall. The challenger offered one to four marbles to be matched by another player, then he tossed the total into the hole from a line about a yard and a half back from the wall. If they all went into the hole, the tosser kept the lot, if an even number went in the hole, the tosser kept them and the non-tosser got the remainder, or if an odd number went in the hole the non-tosser won the lot.

Our hands were always so dirty that when the teacher on playground duty blew a whistle and called 'Get ready for lines', there was no more play and everybody rushed for the washrooms. There were two washrooms each side of the lunch shed and there was also a row of taps and a trough near the bell.

Besides going to the toilet and washing hands, 'Get ready for lines', was a signal for eighty per cent of the pupils who did not wear shoes to collect some Moreton Bay fig leaves to stand on. Not wearing shoes was common because of the economic times, as school photographs show. I never went to school without shoes; in fact, I always had long socks held up with garters. The white elastic left deep red marks about a quarter of an inch wide around my calves; the price paid for being 'a neat little boy'.

The kids without shoes found the bitumen in the centre of the boys' playground too hot to stand on at school assembly during summer, so they would collect a couple of Moreton Bay fig tree leaves to stand on during assembly. Four huge Moreton Bay fig trees grew along the eastern fence of the playground and there were always plenty of leaves on the ground.

That reminds me of Duan Phillips. He was a quiet, timid little boy. I ran into him in later life at an air show. He told me that he had an Aeronautical Engineering degree and that he designed helicopters. The thing he most remembered about Tighes Hill School was standing on Moreton Bay fig leaves when he had bare feet on a summer's day. A lovely story: from no shoes to an aeronautical engineer.

It amazed me how kids just knew it was marble season, because the seasons came and went like migrating birds. Other seasonal activities were kicking a football and hitting a tennis ball with a cricket bat in front of a garbage tin. The most popular playground game was Release. Two captains usually volunteered and an equal number of players was chosen for each team. With no coin to toss, a flat stick or flat stone was spat on one side and 'Wet or Dry?' was called before it was tossed in the air. The losers were the catchers and they drew a large rectangle about six feet by twelve feet with a stick in the playground dirt against a wall while the others ran in all directions. The catchers set off after them and as soon as some were caught, they were placed in prison, which was the drawn rectangle. When a player who was not caught raced through the prison and called 'Release!', the prisoners were free and the catching started all over again. This continued until all prisoners were caught, then the chasers became the chased.

Another game was Hits. Someone was nominated as 'in' and everyone ran around a confined area, usually around a tree, until the person 'in' hit someone with an open hand, then they were 'in'.

Another memory of Third Class was learning to swim. We had to pay two shillings and six pence for lessons at the

Newcastle Ocean Baths in the September school holidays. Sadly, there were only six pupils from Tighes Hill, but we all passed.

In those days, the Newcastle Ocean Baths was one hundred yards by fifty yards and had four lots of steps along the shallow side set in a recess, twelve feet long and three feet wide, with the steps at each end. It was an ideal place for the instructors to have the students swim from one lot of steps to the other in about three feet of water. I remember that learning to swim was anything but pleasant. Lesson one was dog paddling. We had to plunge forward, our hands cupped, going around in furious circles with our chins strained as high as possible. As we all wore woollen swimming costumes covering our chests, the instructor would walk alongside us holding the back shoulder straps to take the weight and give us confidence. After about five one-hour lessons, dog paddling was mastered, so it was time to introduce overarm. At first this was a copy of the dog paddle with heads held high and arms rotating furiously until confidence was gained and we slowly put our faces in the water and had slower and longer strokes. By the end of the second week, we were measuring how many yards we could swim along the side of the baths, five yards, then ten yards, until the final when most of us achieved the goal of twenty-five yards and proudly took our piece of paper home to show our parents.

Over the years, I had a long connection with the Newcastle Ocean Baths: from learning to swim in Third Class, to going to the baths with the school every Friday in primary school and every Wednesday in high school during the summer months on a school sports day.

Our sports afternoon at Newcastle Ocean Baths began with a noisy trip in the tram from Tighes Hill Primary School and later from Newcastle Boys' High School in Waratah, with hundreds of excited kids packed into the old-fashioned trams. The conductor struggled to collect a penny from every passenger. Every kid had three pennies tied in the corner of a handkerchief; one for going in the tram, one for entry into the baths, and one for the tram trip home. We were marched from the tram terminus on the top of the hill down the street to the baths. We then formed a long queue and literally ran through the entrance and threw a penny on the counter, with the attendant scooping them up by the handful and pouring them into his till. A couple of hundred boys dashed through as quickly as possible, and then there was a run to the change room.

During primary school and high school days there were several schools at the baths on a Friday and Wednesday afternoon, so there must have been well over a thousand kids. The dressing area was crowded with boys bumping each other as we put on our swimmers and stuffed our clothes into our school ports (the Newcastle word for cases) then dashed outside. It was so packed that the only way to swim lengths was to hug the sides. I remember swimming the one-hundred-yards length six times without stopping, doing a six-hundred-yard swim. It was my greatest effort.

Kids climbed the tower and jumped in. Very few dived. I was too scared to jump but I loved the high diving board at the side. We put our arms out sideways in mid-air and called it a swallow dive.

Our races on swimming carnival days were all fifty yards. One year, we discovered that the width of the baths had been extended in the swimming lanes and were now fifty metres. I don't remember which year but it was while I was at school.

There was a high wire fence around the outside of the baths and a very high wooden fenced area on the southern end, adjacent to the change rooms. It was about twenty yards by twenty yards and had sand in it. It was for men only to sunbake and many were nude.

One year, the manager placed several brightly coloured round pontoons in the water, about six feet in diameter; they were supported by a couple of drums. I think people were meant to rest on them and sunbake but the school boys invented games of climbing on them and pushing everyone off. It became school versus school and was very active, but good fun.

When it came time to leave, each school was called out at staggered times so there would not be two schools in the dressing rooms at the same time. Newcastle Boys High was called out with a bugle call from one of the cadets. For other schools, the teachers blew whistles or held up signs. It was always a rush, with up to six at a time in the shower. I remember that the change room had a coin-operated Brylcreem dispensing machine. I think it was sixpence, so none of my friends could afford it. Brylcreem was a white substance that kept the hair in place. It was very popular at the time.

Alongside the baths was a huge canoe pool and a smaller 'map of the world' wading pool. I was particularly interested in the map of the world because it had been in the paper that my Geography teacher, Mr Edgar Ford, had been asked by the council to design it. It was thought that Newcastle boys could canoe safely in water about two-feet-six-inches deep and that little kids could pull a toy boat by a string from country to country and learn their geography. However, while the designers knew that changing tides would keep the pools filled with clean sea water, they hadn't expected the deposits of sand with every high tide. Consequently, both the canoe pool and the world pool were constantly being filled with sand. The council had bulldozers and lorries working daily taking sand out of the pools until it became a major expense, and the pools had to be removed.

One of the oldest swimming pools in Newcastle was, and still is, the Bogey Hole south of Newcastle Beach. I was told as a kid that the early convicts cut it out of solid rock, and research recently revealed that it was in fact cut by convicts for Major Morisset in 1819.

It was only in later life when my wife was researching my family history that I discovered that my great grandfather was manager of the Newcastle Ocean Baths in the 1890s.

It was while I was in Third Class that I broke my finger and had an operation to straighten it. It all started when we were camping at Croudace Bay one school holiday and Uncle George, Dad's brother, and his son Georgie, a little older than me, visited us. The boys were 'horsing around' on the grass when I jumped onto Georgie's back. We both staggered backwards and fell on the grass. I put my hand out as I was falling and broke my finger. It was the middle finger of my right hand, and it was bent at right angles across the other fingers. I remember holding my hand on a white handkerchief and sitting on Uncle George's knee in the sidecar as Dad sped in the Harley to Speers Point Ambulance Station. The ambulance man straightened it and put it in a wooden splint and said to see a doctor as soon as possible.

Next day, the doctor said there would have to be an operation to straighten it and asked Mum to prepare a room in our house. That is something that would never happen these days. Mum put a blanket and white sheet on the big table in our glassed-in verandah and draped white sheets over all the chairs stacked at the end. It looked like an operating theatre. Two doctors arrived and put on white gowns and face masks. They laid me on the table and placed cotton wool on my face. I was in my pyjamas and I still remember the images in my mind as I was anesthetised with drops of chloroform from a little brown bottle. I felt like a bee flying deep into a funnel-shaped yellow flower, going lower and lower until it was black. I can still remember it, probably because I have told the story many times.

I woke up in my own bed next morning with a plaster of Paris cast on my middle finger, and as bright as a button, I announced that I wanted go to school to keep my hundred per cent attendance, and to show the kids my finger. Apparently, the doctor said that I could go to school if I felt like it, so I went. I was centre of attention for a day. To end the story, I now have a perfectly straight finger.

Empire Day was held on the 24th of May, Queen Victoria's birthday. Above every schoolroom blackboard was a huge map of the world with the British Empire in red, including Canada, Australia, New Zealand, India, New Guinea, South Africa, and most of the countries in central Africa right up to, but not including, Egypt, with red lines under Malta, Singapore, Hong Kong and Gibraltar, and several islands in the Pacific Ocean. In about 1935 I remember the 'All Red' aeroplane route from Sydney to London being advertised, with the plane stopping at only British Empire airports.

Empire Day was a half-day school holiday, but in the morning, the whole school assembled around the flagpole and we sang patriotic songs. 'God Save the King' was the national anthem in the 1930s. We also sang 'Advance Australia Fair'. Somebody important spoke about the wonderful British Empire then we all went home to prepare our bonfires for Cracker Night. Families met together in backyards and groups congregated on vacant land. Everyone made fires;

some quite big and others in a tin with holes. We all saved for weeks to buy fireworks. A smoke cloud hung over Newcastle, and we could smell smoke in the air.

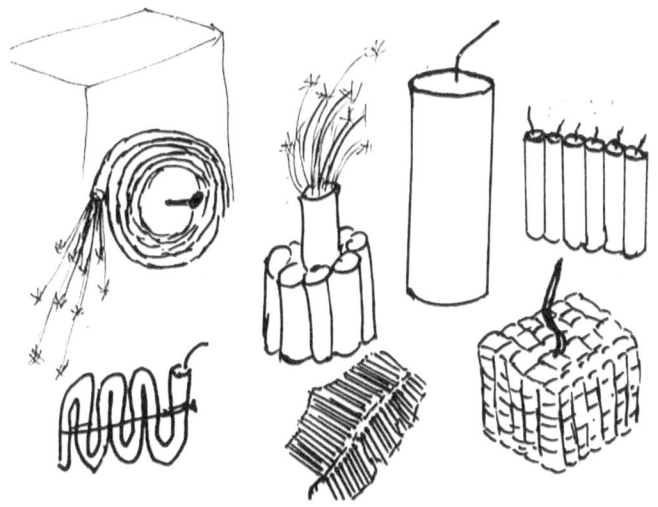

I remember the little Tom Thumbs. They were very small red and green crackers with their wicks woven together so that when the first one was lit, the others followed in sequence like a machine gun. Next were the ten-a-penny bungers, which were red and about a half an inch in diameter and about four inches long. The famous penny bunger was about an inch in diameter and six inches long. Jumping Jacks were light brown and had a series of folds so that when lit they would jump from place to place and explode with every jump. Catherine wheels were round and had to be attached to the fence or a post with a pin in the centre. When lit they spun around shooting out sparks. Flowerpots were a series of small cylinders with a long one in the centre. When lit they put out a string of sparks for quite a while. And, of course, sparklers were always the favourites of the little kids. Basket bombs were two-inch cubes made of woven cane and exploded with a very loud bang. They could completely shatter a wooden letterbox or, unfortunately, a boy's hand, so it is no wonder they are banned today. Then there were 'throw-downs'. These came out on Cracker Night but they were also available throughout the year. They were crackers that did not need a match. They were small paper cylinders about half an inch diameter and half an inch high and twelve came in a paper container with four rows of three. They were packed with lots of very small jagged stones and a small amount of gunpowder. When they were thrown down on a hard surface, apparently the stones rubbed together and made a spark. This ignited the gunpowder and they went off with a loud bang. The idea was to throw them down behind someone to frighten them with the bang. Throw-downs added to the noise of cracker day.

Anzac Day was always celebrated at school on the day before Anzac Day, followed by a holiday on the 25th of April. In the 1930s, Newcastle always had a march up Hunter Street to finish at the marble statue of a soldier opposite Newcastle Post Office, where the Last Post was played. I remember going to town every year and straining to see Uncle George in the procession wearing his soldier's uniform. My father's older brother fought in World War I and marched each year. In the 1930s, the war was still fresh in everyone's mind because many of the returned men were still alive.

Besides Anzac Day and May Day, another annual

procession in Newcastle was the Newcastle Show procession. Our family always lined up with thousands of others on Tudor Street in Hamilton to see the procession pass through on its way to the Show Ground at Broadmeadow. The floats were spectacular. Some lorries were completely covered in flowers with only a small square of glass left on the windscreen for the driver to see out. They were all loaded with pretty girls in skimpy dresses or so it seemed to a wide-eyed schoolboy. Some floats representing a product handed out samples along the way. When the spectators appreciated a float, they all clapped. It was a big event in the Newcastle calendar in the 1930s.

Besides Empire Day, Anzac Day and Newcastle Show Day, Tighes Hill school kids never missed April Fool's Day on the first day of April. It started early in the school day with, 'Your shoelace is undone,' and 'Look over there!', and any other silly thing we could think of; and of course, when someone looked, the victim was called an April Fool by the person giving the false instruction; the unsuspecting victim was laughed at. It was always fun to catch someone, but if it still continued into the afternoon, it was met with: 'Up the tree and down the tree, you're a bigger fool than me. It's after twelve o'clock'. For some reason, catching someone with an April Fool's prank ceased at midday, but in the afternoon, there was 'note pinning'. We pinned notes on fellow students' backs saying, 'Kick Me', and other students obliged until the note was discovered and removed. It was a silly tradition, but it continued every year through the 1930s.

In 1937 I was in Fourth Class, aged nine (I turned ten during the year) with Mr McKinnon. The big event of 1937 was the coronation. Prior to 1937, I was very conscious of George V being king. I had a stamp album and red two-penny George V stamps, as well as green one-penny George V stamps. I don't think I was aware of watermarks at that age; it was later that I started collecting the different watermarks on the backs of them. I remember collecting English stamps with Edward VIII on them with his head facing away from the crown. We all said that he didn't want the crown, so it was no surprise when it was announced that his brother George VI was to be crowned king. All the primary schools in Newcastle went by tram to Number 1 Sports Ground at Cooks Hill. Tighes Hill was the first school to march in, four deep, and I was in the front row. I was the only boy in about a thousand with a cap. I was wearing a brown, houndstooth weave peaked cap.

As we marched around the perimeter of the oval, I heard our family whistle. I must explain; our family had a family whistle. It was virtually three dots and a dash, with a trill in the first three notes. I believe it came from my grandfather who could locate his children in a crowd. It came in handy in 1937 as my mother could see that I was the only boy with a cap. She gave the family whistle, so I ran ahead, passed her my cap over the side fence then returned to my position in the march, much relieved. Then we were directed by our teachers to march on to the centre of the oval and stand between white lines on the grass to form the huge letters spelling out

'GEORGE VI'. The boys all had white shirts and the girls had white dresses. It looked spectacular.

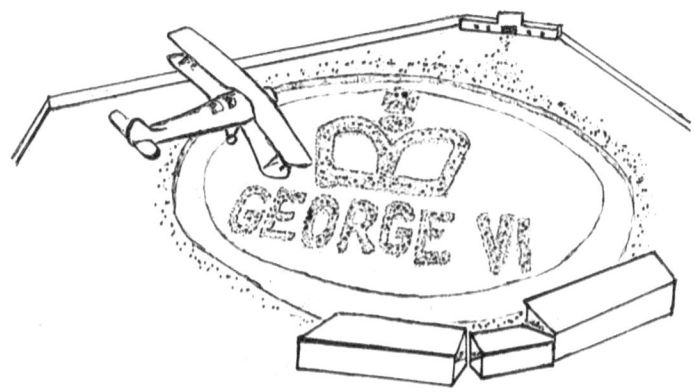

All the children in the Infants' schools were dressed in yellow, and they formed the shape of the cross above the crown, which was drawn on the grass at the top of the display. Then, when we were in position, a Tiger Moth, a biplane from the Newcastle Aero Club, flew over and took our photograph. Next morning it was in the *Newcastle Morning Herald*. I remember also receiving a round chocolate in gold foil, four inches in diameter with the King's head impressed into it. We also received a brown paper bag with an apple, a banana and a sandwich for lunch. It was exciting because it was so unusual for primary school pupils. It was a day in history that I will never forget. (You can find the photograph of the event at the Number 1 Sports Ground taken from the Tiger Moth online.)

While we were in Fourth Class, Elizabeth Street, the gravel street outside the school, was ripped up, rolled flat and covered with bitumen. This involved work with a huge, green steamroller that went up and down while we were at lessons. The noise was deafening. I can remember Mr McKinnon just giving up trying to compete with the noise. He simply said, 'Take out your magazines and read them'.

We couldn't wait to get outside and see this noisy monster. It hissed and puffed and smelled of hot oil. The wheels and roller were huge and it left a smooth flat path wherever it went. We were fascinated with this modern piece of machinery.

Another memory of Fourth Class was being an NRMA boy. Officers from the NRMA came to the school to train six boys to direct the road crossing that was painted on the new bitumen road. I was selected as one of the six and we were given our respective jobs; four boys were to stand on the four corners of the pedestrian crossing opposite the school at 3.30 pm as school came out. The two facing the oncoming traffic were given triangular flags on sticks. We were all given blue NRMA armbands. After the flag boys at the corners had stopped the on-coming traffic with their flags, the two leaders walked across the crossing in opposite directions, one leading a group of school pupils and the other just crossing to be ready for the next batch. The nominated leader who took the children across the road was classmate Neville Princehorn. We were all ten years old and that was 1937, long before lollipop ladies/men replaced us.

After school in the summer, Neville would hurry home on his bike and get dressed in a white double-breasted jacket, put on a small, flat white hat and drive a little ice-cream cart around Tighes Hill. The ice-cream cart was a square little cart with a hood and was drawn by a black pony. Neville sold ice-creams in pink cones with a small scoop for a penny and a large, light-brown cone for thrippence. He rang a bell so that the children would hear him coming. He was always busy. I believe that Neville Princehorn ran a very successful restaurant in Beaumont Street in Hamilton years later.

It was while we were in Fourth Class that Peters Ice Cream gave every school pupil a fifteen-inch, metal-edged ruler with the name 'Peters' on it. They were wonderful. They were on every desk at Tighes Hill School, I presume they were all over New South Wales; they might have been given to every pupil in Australia. It was obviously advertising ice-cream.

They were thicker and heavier than the normal one-penny, twelve-inch ruler. Unfortunately, they were also very handy for teachers to pick up one up and give a sharp rap on a pupils' knuckles, which they did often.

Other memories of Fourth Class include going out into the playground to see an air race. The teachers must have known when they were due over Newcastle, and they took the whole boys' school into the playground to see the Stinson Race. The Stinson was a black and red, single-wing plane and there were five in a race from Brisbane to Sydney. I remember seeing all five planes fly over Newcastle and there was less than a half a mile between first and last. It was an exciting thing to happen in those days.

Other memories include the 'show men' who came to the school with magic tricks, conjuring, balancing acts, and ventriloquists. Because of the Depression, men were desperate for work and went from school to school with these acts for a penny from each pupil, with a halfpenny going to the Parents & Citizens Association (P&C). Any money was appreciated by the P&C so they were always given permission. Most pupils brought their penny and the rest were allowed to go free. I remember many such shows, which were mostly held in the woodwork room. All the woodwork benches were stacked on the verandah and the whole school sat on the floor. One entertainer just made bird calls, animal sounds and mechanical noises with his mouth. He entertained a few classes in the playground under the trees. They were desperate men.

Among the entertainment was a Punch and Judy show. This was a traditional act that first appeared in England in 1660. It is always performed in a sort of red and white striped tent, one yard by one yard and six feet high. One or two people crammed inside the tent and operated the puppets in a small stage-like opening at the front. The script was always the same and by the time I had seen the show at school, at the Railway picnics and Newcastle Beach at a summer carnival, it was getting a bit boring. The 1930s was the era of Punch and Judy in Newcastle.

Besides having these entertainers, the P&C also raised money with Toffee Days. Mothers were asked to make a tray of toffee. They were always in round cupcake paper containers, and the son or daughter of the person who made them carried them around the playground on a tray, selling them for a penny each. This happened once or twice a year.

I remember the rush to the little shop next to the school at lunchtime, as well as to the fish and chips shop. I never bought my lunch for the whole of my school life but many did. A cone of hot chips was a penny and that was the most popular at the shop on the opposite side of the road. The favourite lunch for the rich kids was a cream horn, which was a puff-pastry cone filled with cream. I think it was thrippence.

Mr McKinnon taught us Nature Study. We were taught the parts of a flower as well as the different types of dogs, horses and birds. It was very basic but interesting; it made us aware of things in nature. The best part was that we had to draw each one, and the class judged the best drawing by clapping loudly. Mr McKinnon gave the winner thrippence. I proudly won it several times, one of which was placed in the Newcastle Show as representing Newcastle primary schools. It was a big deal for a little kid.

In the half-yearly exams in Fourth Class I came fourth in the class and sat at the back on the extreme left-hand side of the classroom with the 'good kids': Warren McGregor, Athol Armbrister and Bavin Evans. I remained friends with these fellows until well into retirement.

It was while I was in Fourth Class that I had my school holidays at Blackalls, visiting my cousins Jack and Joyce Attwood. My grandparents were often visiting at the same time. It was before my grandfather had retired from teaching. My grandmother spoiled her grandchildren by often giving us a penny each, which we would immediately take to the Blackalls shop and buy a penny Nestles chocolate. This was a thin, four inches by two inches chocolate in a red wrapper, but inside was a picture of something special. We were encouraged to save these in a book that was printed to collect twelve pictures in each of the twelve pages. The ones I liked the most were of Ancient Egypt. I collected all twelve and read about this interesting place.

By coincidence, about the same time there was a series of articles in the *Newcastle Morning Herald* entitled 'Into the Land of Egypt' written by H.V. Morton. Dad read them each night to my brother and me after tea. I was fascinated with them. I am sure that my boyhood fascination prompted me and my wife to go on a boat trip down the Nile in my retirement, and we visited every temple in Egypt. We also flew out to Abu Simbel and saw the temple built by Ramses II. I have a photograph that I took of Abu Simbel on my living room wall. And it all started with a penny chocolate in 1937.

I was in Fifth Class in 1938. Our teacher was Mr Matherson, who just happened to be the brother of Max Matherson, one of our classmates, but no preferential treatment was ever given. Mr Matherson threw chalk at pupils not paying attention. He was the only one of our teachers who did this.

One day at the beginning of class when Mr Matherson was writing up the roll, he asked every pupil, in alphabetical order, their full name including their second name. When he came to Billy Knight, he said, 'Stand up. What is your full name, including your second name?'

Billy replied, 'Billy William Knight!' The whole class burst out laughing. Mr Matherson said, 'Are you serious?' Billy replied, 'Yes, sir. My grandparents call me William and my parents call me Billy, so I thought I had two names.' The class doubled-up with laughter. Everyone except Billy could see the funny side of it. He was called 'Billy William' for the rest of his school life. Kids can be cruel.

Even though we had 'hat rooms', which was an area at the entrance to each classroom with rows of hat pegs, hardly any boy wore a hat to school in the 1930s, but we wore hats at weekends. At one stage, straw hats were popular. Kids called them donkey breakfasts. They were cheap and did not last long. In about 1938 there was a sudden influx of topees. These were a moulded straw hat shaped like the English pith helmet, with a cloth lining containing an adjustable elastic cord so that one size fit all. They were extremely popular but the craze only lasted a year or two, then they disappeared.

Very early in 1938, we were told that this year was Australia's sesqui-centenary year, that is, 150 years since Australia was founded in 1788, so PE instructors were sent to all Newcastle primary schools to train us in flag drill. I think we had flags right from the start to keep us interested and I can always remember doing exercises to music, so they probably had portable wind-up gramophones. We were organised into well-spaced lines and had to sing, 'One and two, three and four ...', right up to sixteen while doing a set of arm exercises in unison. When the big day arrived, we all had to wear white shirts and black pants and the girls had white dresses (there were no school uniforms in those days). Dozens of trams took every Newcastle primary school to Number 1 Sports Ground, as we did in 1937 for the coronation.

When we were marched onto the grass oval, we saw a huge 150 painted on the grass, and the teachers marched a thousand kids into position. Tighes Hill was at the top of the '0' in the 150. When everyone was in place, a Tiger Moth from the Newcastle Aero Club flew over and took our photograph, which was in the *Newcastle Morning Herald* the next morning.

Next came what must have been a logistical nightmare for the teachers; the one thousand primary school pupils had to be spread out over the whole oval in straight lines in two directions and all two yards apart. There were white lines on the grass and they achieved it in a very short time. Then the music began over a loudspeaker and we all sang, 'One and two; three and four ...' while doing arm movements and lunging forward. We had the Union Jack in our left hand and the Australian flag in our right hand. Incidentally, the Australian flag was red and not blue in those days. It looked spectacular with a thousand flags all moving together, and the noise of the movement was like wind rushing through trees. It was an unforgettable memory! Then we were lined up to receive our brown paper bag with our lunch, as well as a four-inch diameter gold, foil-covered chocolate with a picture of Arthur Phillip's head. We were also given a book with Governor Arthur Phillip on the cover and pictures inside of explorers and important Australian people.

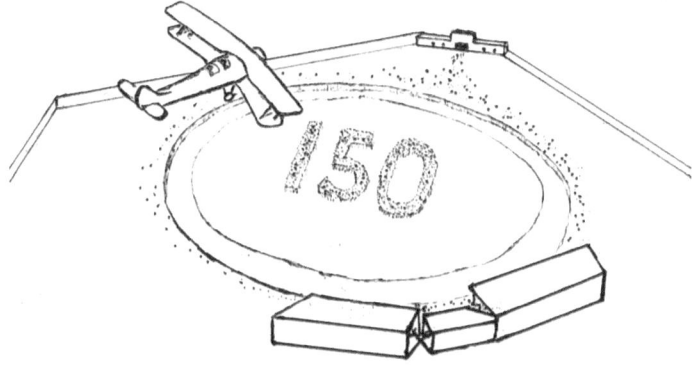

Fifth Class seemed to stress English History. I remember long charts hanging from the ceiling with rows of dates and events such as, 1215 Magna Carta, 1265 First Parliament, and so on.

It was in Fifth Class that we measured the shadow of a stick at midday. Between the woodwork room and the Infants' school there was a concrete circle one yard in diameter with a pole in the centre. Every day at twelve o'clock, Bavin Evans left the classroom and measured the shadow of the stick. He announced the length when he returned to the classroom and we all wrote it in the back of our Geography book. It made us aware of the seasons.

We were only in Fifth Class for one term when the principal, Mr Stove, came in and said, 'There are too many pupils in this class.'

We had desks right to the blackboard.

'We will have to put six boys up into Sixth Class. They are the six top boys: Warren McGregor, Athol Armbrister, Bavin Evans, Richard Grimmond, Neville Davis and Jim Beath.'

I spent the rest of that year doing sixth-class work. Arithmetic was hard. Our teacher was Mr Stove and he taught Arithmetic with a cane in his hand. After every group of ten sums he caned everyone who got less than five correct. I received the cane frequently so I learnt sixth-class arithmetic very quickly.

English, I managed, but I came top in History and Geography at the end of the year, after only two terms in Sixth Class. I was proud of that, but we were not allowed to go to high school at the end of the year because we were too young, so all six of us repeated Sixth Class. It was only to reduce the numbers of students in Fifth Class.

We were taught Technical Drawing and Woodwork in Sixth Class. We had to buy a 2H and a HB pencil and an Art Gum rubber that cost one shilling. I liked Technical Drawing. Never did I imagine at the time, that I would be a Technical Drawing teacher for most of my working life.

It was while I was in Sixth Class that I discovered the Australian author Ion Idriess, and I read as many of his books as I could find in the school library.

Other memories of school include riding a bike to school. Only a few kids rode bikes, everyone else walked. I can absolutely assure pupils today that in my day, NOT ONE pupil was driven to my school. That is a luxury that future generations invented. I walked from Queens Road and when my parents purchased a new house in Islington, I walked to school in Fourth Class in 1937, but rode my bike in Fifth and Sixth Class in 1938 and 1939.

Not only did I ride the bike, I also 'doubled' my younger brother. To double someone or 'double-dink', as it was called, was to carry them on the crossbar that ran from the seat to the handlebars. The passenger sat sideways, with legs hanging down, with body twisted and with hands gripping the handlebar near the centre. It was quite common in the 1930s, but is rarely seen today.

Speaking of bikes, even at a young age I was taught to mend my own punctures. This involved removing the tyre with tyre levers, filling the tube with air and holding it below the surface in a dish of water to locate the stream of bubbles. The hole was circled with an indelible pencil (a special pencil that was purple and could not be rubbed out on paper). The area was dried, rubber glue applied from a tube, and a patch was pressed in position. After given time to dry, it was placed inside the tyre.

We all learned this process very young through necessity, as 'cats' heads' were common. These were a hard pointed seed from a weed that grew in long grass. Besides small pinpoint punctures, we also had 'blow-outs'. This was when we wore down the tread on the tyre until it exposed the inner tube. If we didn't notice it soon enough and got a new tyre then the tube wore through and exploded with a bang.

This needed a vulcanised patch. These came in kits in a rectangular tin with a lid that was perforated with raised points used to roughen the surface of the rubber tube where the patch was to go. After roughening the rubber around the hole, the patch that was on a tin holder was clamped over the hole using a clamp. The clamp was G-shaped and had a thread that tightened and pressed the patch to the tube. A cardboard-like material within the oval patch holder was scratched with a screwdriver then set alight with a match. It burnt vigorously, producing volumes of smoke and providing the heat that vulcanised the oval rubber patch to the tube. After allowing fifteen to twenty minutes for it to cool, the clamp was released and a red oval patch was firmly adhered to the tube.

Chapter 4   School

Besides mending punctures, I also oiled my bike and adjusted the cones regularly. Under Dad's supervision, I painted my bike, which was not uncommon in the 1930s. Firstly, I dismantled it completely, putting nuts, washers, cotter pins and ball-bearings in separate little tins. Then I removed the old paint with emery cloth, coarse first then fine, until the frame was shiny steel. First coat was metal primer, followed by white undercoat then red enamel. I hung it up with wire hooks attached to the shed rafters to dry. After it was reassembled, I went to the bike shop and bought transfers. The most popular at the time was the 'rose transfer', so I put roses on the main frame as well as each side of the front forks. As strange as it seems now, it was perfectly normal for the 1930s, and I was proud of the result.

Incidentally, second-hand bikes were one pound and a new bike was four pounds, which was more than my father's weekly wage.

In 1937 when I was walking home from Tighes Hill to Islington, I varied my route and sometimes came along Maitland Road, the Pacific Highway. On the southern side of Maitland Road, near the Baptist Church, was a blacksmith's workshop. I remember seeing a horse being shod in Newcastle in the 1930s. I hung on the slip-rails watching him. Slip-rails were two smooth saplings about nine feet long and four inches in diameter that served as a gate. They slotted into two vertical posts just less than nine feet apart. The blacksmith was a big fellow with huge arms, wearing a black singlet and sweating profusely. He worked over a coke fire that made his face glow.

There was always a special smell at the blacksmith's forge. He lifted up the huge hoof of the big draught-horse and rested it on his knee with his back to the horse. He filed it vigorously until he had a pile of white shavings on the ground and a flat foot. He kept pumping a long wooden handle that operated the leather bellows to make the fire glow. He also kept repositioning the red-hot horseshoe that was buried in the red coals until it was glowing red hot. He took it out with tongs and held it about an inch away from the horse's hoof to check the size. He positioned it on the horn of his anvil and gently tapped it to make it a fraction smaller. Then he tested it against the hoof again. When he was satisfied that the size was right, he pressed the red-hot horseshoe into the hoof, producing clouds of white smoke that made the line of kids cough and turn their heads.

'Doesn't that hurt the horse?' called a small voice.

'No, it doesn't hurt a bit! It makes a flat bed,' called out the blacksmith. He always shouted. Then, when satisfied with the size, he plunged the red-hot horseshoe into a bucket of water, making a loud hiss and clouds of steam. Next, he laid the cold horseshoe in the black groove. Then, taking a handful of nails out of his apron pocket and holding them between his leathery lips, he took them one at a time and nailed the steel horseshoe onto the horse's hoof.

'No, he doesn't feel it!' he called out over the din, anticipating a question from the audience. Then he dropped the hoof and straightened up, rubbing his back. We were privileged to see it, as he was probably the last commercial blacksmith in Newcastle, although the Newcastle Co-op and

Dark's Ice Works had a team of horses for their carts, so they probably had their own blacksmiths. I often tell people about seeing a working blacksmith on the way home from school in the 1930s. It is real history.

After being together since primary school, some firm friendships were formed over the years, but these were to be shattered when we split up for our respective high schools. We had a primary school final exam. This was a public examination set by the Department of Education for all primary schools, but we also had an IQ test and I really believe that this determined which high school we were sent to. It was common knowledge that Newcastle Boys High School was a 'selective' high school for potential doctors, lawyers and teachers, while the newly opened Newcastle Technical High School at Tighes Hill was for potential engineers and other technical careers. Cooks Hill Intermediate High School in town taught bookkeeping and was for students going into the commercial world. Pupils from Cooks Hill Intermediate High School could continue Fourth and Fifth Year at Newcastle Boys High if they passed their Intermediate Certificate.

Newcastle Junior High School, in the centre of town, was for the less academic, while Central Intermediate High School at Broadmeadow was a boys' school for tradesmen and general occupations.

So, the Tighes Hill sixth class was split up among the five Newcastle high schools. Four Tighes Hill primary school students were assigned to Newcastle Boys High School with me so some friendships continued for another five years.

On a different tack, could the 'sense of humour' of a whole nation change from decade to decade? In the 1930s, there was a craze of 'Little Audrey' jokes as well as 'Knock-Knock' jokes. I thought they were stupid at the time and still do, but they 'gripped the nation'. In the Little Audrey jokes, someone gets killed, run over by a steamroller, or is burnt in a house fire and Little Audrey 'laughed and laughed' virtually because she knew it was going to happen. They were macabre to say the least, but they persisted for a decade. And then there were 'Knock, Knock' jokes; and they seemed to last the whole of the 1930s ... they went on forever. Again, I don't see why people thought they were funny; perhaps I do not have a 1930s' sense of humour. A typical knock-knock joke was:

'Knock, knock.'
'Who's there?'
'Arch.'
'Arch, who?'
'Bless you.'

And so they went on and on for years. Goodness knows why!

Chapter 4   School

In 1978, I heard about the Tighes Hill Public School centenary celebration, one hundred years from 1878 to 1978, so I decided to attend. I was principal of Finley High School at the time. I sent a copy of my school photographs in advance as requested. After attending the official function and listening to the speeches, the public was invited to the photographic exhibition. It was while looking at these, that a fellow visitor was commenting on my 1936 photograph and between us we were naming all the pupils.

'That is little Max Valentine!' I said, pointing to a little red-haired boy, and the strapping big fellow beside me said, 'That's ME!'

So, after a happy revival of friendship, we agreed to arrange a class reunion. Max and I used the Newcastle telephone book to contact almost every pupil of the class of 1938. We met at the school and were invited to use our old fourth-class room, which is now the library. We posed for a photograph then had an escorted tour of the school. We were amused that the room that was once the principal's office is now the indoor toilet.

We agreed to have regular reunions and I was given the task of organising them. We always had them in the Railway Carriage Shed in the Foreshore Park, which was a public park behind the old Newcastle train station. There was good cover and plenty of room. We had several Tighes Hill School reunions over the years, right up to our 70th in 2009. Because Arthur Gibbons married Betty Curtis, also a pupil of that era, she was able to contact the girls, and the following reunions also included the girls. We had over fifty at our 70th

Tighes Hill reunion in 2009. There was good coverage in the *Newcastle Herald* of the Class of 1939.

One by one I heard of the deaths of our fellow pupils, and now I am the only Tighes Hill boy from the Sixth Class of 1939 still alive.

CHAPTER 5

Sunday School

Sunday School played a big part in my life by developing attitudes and values. It was the network of all my friends and social life, occupying a large portion of my time growing up in the 1930s.

I was told that I was taken to Tighes Hill Methodist Sunday School at age three and I attended regularly for fifteen years but decided to have other interests from age eighteen onwards.

Contrary to what you may expect, I was not what may be termed 'religious'; in fact, I was the opposite. While I accepted the Christian philosophy, I questioned the details. However, I enjoyed the friendships made at Sunday School.

Being a Methodist in the 1930s carried a certain expectation of behaviour. In general, Methodists were very conservative, in that they attended their church regularly, did not drink alcohol, nor did they attend public dances; goodness knows why. We did not play cards on a Sunday or even go for a swim. I never remember hearing my mother swear, or for that matter, any of her family, her sisters or my grandparents.

From a very early age, my brother and I said grace before every meal, as did all my relations. Between about age three to six I remember my brother and I holding the palms of our hands together and saying, 'For what we are about to receive, we are truly thankful'. From about the age of six, we did not put our hands together, or close our eyes, but we simply bowed our heads with eyes downcast and looking reverent while saying grace, right up to the time we were teenagers. It was the 'norm' for Methodist families in the 1930s. I can remember that we even said grace on family picnics at Newcastle Beach on a Saturday in summer; and naturally our cousins said it also.

Of all the Methodist influences, the only one that remained with me was my aversion to alcohol.

Tighes Hill Sunday School had four 'departments' in the 1930s. There was kindergarten for the under-fives. They had a room for themselves with dedicated teenage teachers who gave them games and read stories. Then there was a group with children aged five to ten. I remember that they had the 'Birthday Chair'. When it was someone's birthday, they sat in the Birthday Chair, and we all sang 'Happy Birthday'. The Sunday School teachers were dedicated young people of the church and told their weekly story using a 'sand-tray'. This was a square dish filled with sand and used as a focal point while a story was told. A small twig was used as a tree and the people in the story were represented by wooden matches. They held the attention of the listener.

I remember the 'collection', when someone took a long-handled basket around and everyone put a penny in it while we sang, 'Hear the pennies dropping! Listen to them fall. Every one for Jesus, He shall have them all!' I remember thinking, if He is in Heaven, how is he going to get the pennies?

Just before we went home, the teachers gave us each a Sunday School card. This was a little card with a religious picture and a verse on it. We carefully saved these and when we had six, we brought them back and got a bigger card, which also had a religious picture and a verse. And finally, six of these were rewarded with a very big card with a religious picture and a verse. I received several of these.

Then there was another department called the Junior Department, with children aged between ten and fifteen. Mr Fisher, the local bootmaker, was in charge of that department. There was always a collection and the plate went around and every child put in a penny. The adults put in a thrippence, which is why the Australian slang for a thrippence was a 'tray bit'.

The seniors, aged fifteen to seventeen, sat in the church seats in two or three groups of four or five. So, in all there were at least fifty children attending Tighes Hill Methodist Sunday School in the 1930s. Some came from Mayfield, the adjoining suburb. Over the years the numbers dwindled until it folded altogether and no longer exists.

In the 1930s, there was also a Church of England Sunday School in Tighes Hill, as well as a big Roman Catholic Church in Union Street. There was a strong prejudice against Catholics in the 1930s. I saw Tighes Hill school kids throwing stones at the Catholic pupils going past their school in the 1930s. And this was Australia, not Ireland.

Methodists, a Protestant denomination, was very strong in Newcastle in the 1930s. There were large numbers in the congregations in Tighes Hill, Mayfield, Hamilton, and Adamstown, as well as the City Mission in King Street in the city. There were so many active Methodist churches in Newcastle that we held our own sports day, with age races, high jumps, and tug-of-war contests that occupied a whole day.

The Order of Knights also conducted camps at Dungog Showground. We slept in the pavilion on straw-filled hessian bags and went swimming in the river. In most Methodist churches there was a 'secret' boys' club called the Order of Knights. It was based on high moral principles and copied King Arthur's Knights of the Round Table. There was a secret handshake and a secret password. It was based on the Masonic Lodge. I held several officer positions in the Order of Knights over the years and enjoyed it. Looking back, all of these associations shaped values, developed personalities, and formed friendships that lasted a lifetime.

I have a photograph of Dad in the Tighes Hill Methodist Church choir. There were over forty people in the church choir alone. There would have been four times that many in the general congregation. Church attendance was strong in the 1930s. Within the church there were strong social bonds between members. We had many social nights and concerts at Tighes Hill Methodist Church in the 1930s. There were singers and piano players at church concerts, and there was never a shortage of acts. It was an era when we entertained each other.

At that time, tap dancing was popular. This was a rhythmic foot shuffle with aluminium toes on the shoes, which made a loud tapping noise. Fancy dress frolics were popular also. I remember going dressed as Charlie Chaplin, wearing a bowler hat and long, baggy trousers. I think my moustache was boot polish. I won first prize for that costume and I received a Conway Stewart propelling pencil, quite a prestigious item for those times.

I remember the silent black-and-white Charlie Chaplin movies in the church hall. We thought they were wonderful because it was modern technology at that time. It was the era before TV and people mixed and talked and laughed together. The church was our network of friends.

I must explain social nights at the Methodist Church Hall and the games we played, as they would be so different to modern socials. We always had a MC, or Master of Ceremonies, and he announced the games. There would be about fifty people attending, ranging in age from five to eighteen, with a few parents who mainly sat together and watched.

'Over the broom' was always popular. A large circle was formed with boy-girl pairs, some holding hands, and the piano played a noisy march. The boy-girl pairs started walking briskly around in a circle with couples stepping over a hair broom that had been placed on the floor across the circle. After everyone was marching to the music in a happy mood, the playing stopped abruptly and the whole circle stopped moving. The last couple to have stepped over the broom were 'out', and the MC directed them to their seats at the side. Everyone laughed, some clapped, and the music started up again and the circle moved off.

And, would you believe? This would go on for half an hour until only two or three couples remained. The interest was intense with everyone watching to see who would be last. Finally, only two couples would be hurrying around the circle with everyone watching eagerly. The time between stops was deliberately extended. Everyone was standing around the outside of the circle and finally when the music stopped, a winner was declared and there was happy clapping and congratulations given.

Next was 'musical chairs'. The MC and helpers would line up about ten chairs in two rows of five, back-to-back. A rush of volunteers would form a circle around the chairs, sometimes only boys and sometimes only girls. The MC would select the number of players and the piano started playing while the people walked around the chairs. When the music stopped there was a rush to sit on a chair, but only ten were seated. Amid much laughter, all those without a chair walked back to their seats at the side and sat down. The MC would remove one chair until there were ten players and only nine chairs. The music continued until the MC signalled the pianist and it stopped abruptly. There was a frantic rush for the chairs but one person would miss out on finding a chair. The MC would direct them to a seat at the side, and so it would go on until only two people circled one chair. Everyone watched anxiously until finally the music stopped and there was a rush for the last chair and one person was declared the winner.

Next was 'twos and threes'. The MC would organise a circle of couples facing inwards. Two people were selected as runner and catcher, and one would chase the other. He or she would run around the outside of the circle with the other player chasing them. Then the person being chased would suddenly move to the inner circle and stand in front of a couple, forming three. The person at the back was then being chased and ran quickly around the outside of the circle. To avoid being caught they would stand in front of a couple making three, and the back person was then the one being chased ... and so on. The object of the game was to catch the runner, then the positions were reversed and the runner became the catcher. Again, this would go on for at least half an hour, until everyone was exhausted and needed a rest.

Then there was 'spin the bottle'; of course, it was a soft drink bottle. The MC would get everybody into the centre of the room and then he would spin a bottle in the centre. When the bottle stopped spinning around, the neck pointed a certain direction. The MC would direct a quarter of the people to return to their seats. As the numbers reduced, he was able to spread them evenly in a circle. After a few more spins, there was only one left, the winner.

Another party game was, 'O'Grady says!'. The MC would line up the players and stand in front of them saying, 'O'Grady says "hands up"'. And everyone would raise their hands above their heads. When the MC said, 'Hands down', all those who put their hands down were 'out' because O'Grady did not say it. With much laughter, those people would return to their seats. The MC continued with orders, some with 'O'Grady says' and some not. All those who responded when O'Grady did not say it, were 'out' until only one remained, the winner.

It may seem so childish now but it was normal in the 1930s and everyone enjoyed a social night. People mixed together, laughed together, boy-girl shyness was overcome and friendships were formed.

Incidentally, Methodists never had dances, when all over Newcastle, dance halls were common. No ballroom dancing was a policy and every Methodist church adhered to it. Methodists did not drink alcohol, and when I tell people that I have never had an alcoholic drink in ninety-six years they are astounded, but it was normal for those times. None of my family or friends ever had alcohol in the house or consumed it socially or privately. I tell people that that is why my mind is so alert at my age. It probably has no scientific basis, but I get a kick out of it.

Actually, my strong aversion to alcohol was reinforced when observing the 'six o'clock swill' from our Islington house. When I was growing up in the 1930s the law forced hotels to close at 6 pm. This was very noticeable on Saturdays. At 6 pm we could hear the barman across the road from our house calling, 'Everybody out!' Then about fifty to one hundred drunken men would spill into Maitland Road and stagger in all directions, with some spewing, others fighting, while most sat in the gutter not knowing where their home was. This was such a shocking scene every Saturday that it left an everlasting impression on me, but it was typical of every hotel in Newcastle in the 1930s.

Methodists were very devoted to their church and many attended Sunday morning church at 11 am, with Sunday School from 2.30 to 3.30 pm and church again at 7 pm. Everyone wore their best clothes and boys used brilliantine, a hair oil, on their hair. This was a product of the era to be replaced later by Brylcreem in the late 1930s. I think the brand I used was called Californian Poppy. It was the norm and all the boys used it to look neat and smell 'nice'.

The highlight of the year for the children was the annual Sunday School picnic. This involved hiring several buses (in those days the Newcastle double-decker green bus) and going to a Lake Macquarie picnic park, usually Speers Point. They always had a happy atmosphere. There were age races, lollies and ginger beer, as well as a picnic lunch – a novelty in Depression times.

Another highlight of the church year was the anniversary, which was an annual celebration of the beginning of that particular church. It was celebrated by decking the church with flowers and learning special songs. Some children recited or sang, and book prizes were given to children for good attendance. I received a book every year. Besides the Sunday

School anniversary, I remember celebrating the Harvest Festival each year with a display of fruit and vegetables in front of the altar. Someone, or a committee, made a special effort to make this look spectacular. I think it rivalled the Royal Easter Show in Sydney. I remember many large sheaves of wheat, something very foreign to Tighes Hill, being the main feature. I have no idea where they came from. Then there were different fruits and vegetables displayed, some years in heaped baskets and in other years they were spread over a flat surface with divisions, but always depicting a land of plenty. I remember that the apples were always highly polished. I guess it expressed our gratitude for the land giving us food. There was always a happy atmosphere at Harvest Festival and a sense of celebration. It was a feature of the 1930s.

The Sunday School also celebrated Mother's Day. Everyone wore a white carnation and the church was decorated with white flowers. There were special services for mothers and some children learnt poems about mothers.

Our Tighes Hill church also had a fete during the year to raise money. This was announced well in advance so people could get started making things for the stalls. On the day, always a Saturday, stalls were set up around the hall to display the donated goods. There was the scones-and-cake stall giving the ladies an opportunity to produce beautiful scones and iced cakes. Then there was the donated second-hand clothing and knitted wear, all to raise money for the church.

I remember Sundays for another reason. It was 'bath day'. I'm not kidding! In the 1930s most of the population had only one bath per week, some had even fewer. It was normal, probably because most of us were only one or two generations from the English who came from a colder country and those of English heritage followed the habits of their parents and grandparents.

We had our weekly bath on Sunday before lunch, so we could put on our good clothes and go to Sunday School. Of course, there was no hot water systems or even bath heaters in the average home. Hot water had to be carried from the stove to the bath in the kettle and several saucepans. Some people used a four-gallon kerosene tin partly filled, because it would be too heavy to lift from the stove filled with four gallons of water. My mother had a smaller red tin about ten inches in diameter and eighteen inches high, which she carried by the small tabs around the top.

Although we never owned one, some people had a chip heater for heating bath water in the 1930s. It was a chrome cylinder about a foot in diameter and two feet high, with a six-inch chimney that went through the roof. It stood on three legs and had a shower attached as well as a long spout that directed the hot water into the bath. There was a six-inch-diameter, circular opening on the top through which the fuel was added. Ideally, it heated the water by burning finely chopped wood kindling, but most people used copious sheets of newspaper. The temperature of the water was regulated by adjusting the flow with the tap. A very slow flow gave hotter water but took a long time to fill a bath.

I must tell you how 'advertising' changed the culture of

people in the 1930s. In every paper and magazine there was an advertisement for Lifebuoy, a carbolic soap. The cake of soap was red and had squared corners. The advertising was in the form of a two-picture comic. The first picture showed a man or a woman at a party or social gathering being isolated because they had 'BO' (body odour). The last picture showed them popular and the life of the party because someone had told them about Lifebuoy soap. I really believe that this advertisement accelerated evolving attitudes that changed society and most people bathed more regularly in the 1940s.

CHAPTER 6

Toys and Games

The first toy I can remember was a set of nine wooden building blocks, each a two-inch cube. When placed in a special order, three blocks by three blocks, there was a nursery rhyme picture on each of the six faces; but I preferred building towers.

Another very early toy I remember was a clockwork dirigible. I called it my 'airship'. It was a tin-plated, cigar-shaped model flying machine about twelve inches long and three inches in diameter. Dad attached two lengths of string and hung it on a hook from the ceiling of the back verandah. When wound up, propellers drove it around in a circle. Dirigibles were a form of travel in the early 1930s. It was well before the tragic 1937 dirigible disaster (Hindenburg, the German dirigible, was the largest rigid airship ever constructed. In 1937 it caught fire and was destroyed; thirty-six people died).

I also had a celluloid horse and rider. It was about eight inches long and was clockwork. When wound up with its key, it pranced or jumped around and the rider, a knight in armour, waved a sword. Dad called him 'de Groot' because that was the name of the man who used a sword to cut the ribbon at the 1932 opening of the Sydney Harbour Bridge before Premier Jack Lang cut it with scissors. De Groot was dressed in an officer's uniform and brazenly rode his horse in front of the Premier. Of course, de Groot was arrested, the ribbon replaced, and Jack Lang officially cut it again. The papers were full of it; de Groot was a member of the New Guard, a right-wing movement opposed to Jack Lang's Labor policies. Jack Lang was very popular with the Labor voters but when he would not pay the interest on the State loans from the Commonwealth, he was dismissed from office in 1932 by the New South Wales governor, Philip Game. Politics were in turmoil in the 1930s.

But back to my toys. Most toys were operated by winding up a spring, as in a clock, so they were called clockwork toys. Toy cars, trains, and anything that moved was clockwork. And they were ALL made in Japan.

A very popular toy of the era was the pop-pop boat. This was a colourful tin-plate boat about six inches long that was driven by a short candle placed under the cabin. The candle heated water passing through two thin tubes that caused the boat to make a 'pop pop' sound and to be propelled at a brisk rate around a tub of water.

Girls always had dolls and doll houses. Rich kids had a rocking horse, which was a beautifully carved horse about three feet long with realistic hair for the mane and tail.

Small children rode a stick with a wooden horse head and two wheels at the back. Rich kids had pedal cars, and three-wheel bikes were common. I had a second-hand, three-wheel bike that my cousin George Grimmond grew too big for. My pride and joy was a Number Three Meccano set. It  cost my mother three pounds ten shillings, a week's wages for Dad in 1936. Over the following years I built cranes and towers and everything in the book that came with it. I am sure that it gave me mechanical skills that I used in later life. I used it right up to my teenage years and kept it for many, many years before selling it recently for three hundred dollars. My son and grandsons also used it as they were growing up. It was a wonderful toy.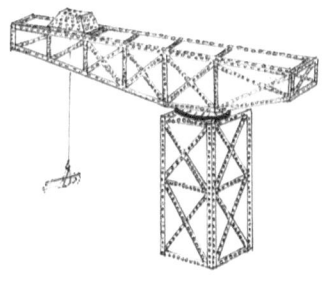

Other toys of the era included yo-yos and tops. Yo-yos were round wooden toys that were spun by winding a string on a small axle, holding the string around a finger and throwing it down hard to make it spin. There were demonstrations outside newsagencies on Saturday mornings to promote sales. Some boys at my school became very clever and could do several tricks. Yo-yos were introduced into Australia from America in the 1930s. Tops, on the other hand, were passed on from the 1920s through their parents.

Tops were small conical wooden shapes with a steel point. String was wound carefully up the cone and when it was thrown down, the string was jerked back causing the top to spin. Tops were allowed in the school playground and we played games called 'pegging', where we tried to knock another player's spinning top out of a circle drawn in the playground.

Smaller children had colourful, metal tops about a foot in diameter, which were operated by pumping a handle up and down. Not really a toy, the shanghai, like the top, was passed on from the 1920s and most fathers or big brothers

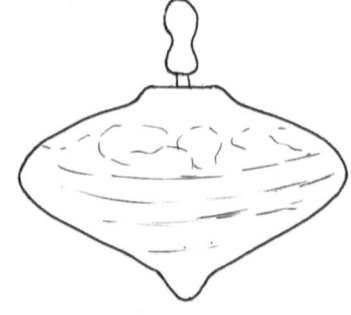

showed the next generation how to make them. Firstly, a forked stick was selected, usually from a gum-tree, and cut to size. Two rubber lengths were cut from a car inner tube, and the leather pad that held the stone was always the tongue of an old boot.

The skill in attaching the rubber to the forked stick was to stretch the rubber before binding string tightly around it; likewise with the leather boot tongue. My father showed me how to make a shanghai in the 1930s and I became a 'good shot' at hitting jam tins. No, I didn't fire at birds; I had paid sixpence to belong to the Gould League of Bird Lovers and had a framed card on my dressing table to prove it.

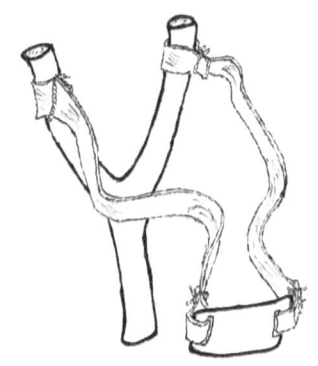

Also, not really a toy, was a pocketknife. At some stage most kids owned one and they could whittle wood, sharpen pencils, and carve their names on a tree, as well as peel apples.

Another homemade toy was the cotton reel steamroller. This was an ordinary wooden cotton reel with an elastic band threaded through the

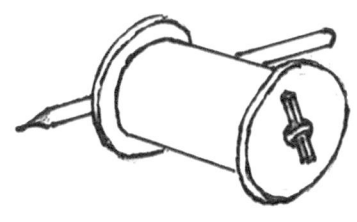

hole in the centre and held in place with half a wooden match one end and a long pencil the other. The pencil was wound around until the elastic band was tight. When placed on the floor, the cotton reel raced along using the energy in the wound-up band. My brother and I raced these along the back verandah.

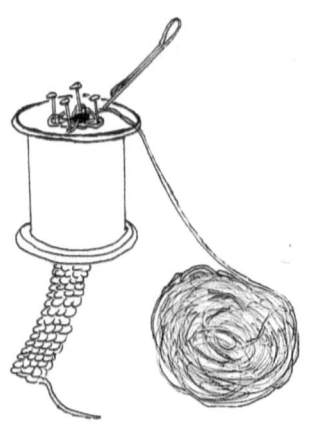

More of an activity than a toy was French knitting. Girls in the 1930s often engaged in French knitting. This was done on a wooden cotton reel by first fixing four small nails around the hole on one end. Wool was then wound around the nails and knitting stitches were formed by lifting the wool over the nail heads with a bobby pin to form knitting stitches. Slowly, a knitted 'tube' came out of the other end. Long lengths of French knitting were then sewn in circles to make a teapot stand or for the more industrious, a larger mat or a beanie.

In the 1930s every kid at some time made a jam-tin telephone. This was two empty jam tins connected with a long length of string coming from a hole in the centre of each tin. With the string pulled taught and one tin held to the ear at one end, another person spoke into the second tin. The voice was supposed to travel along the string. I was not thoroughly convinced it worked, but every kid tried it.

At some stage every kid discovers a magnifying glass, probably received as a birthday present. Children can be fascinated looking at flowers, dead flies, and grains of sugar, but most intriguing was focusing sunshine to a small bright spot that concentrated the sun's rays to burn wood and even write a name on a piece of wood. Naughty children were often guilty of burning live ants to their death with a magnifying glass.

Then there were kites. Most children had a go at making kites. Kites were two crossed pieces of different lengths of wood, tied at right 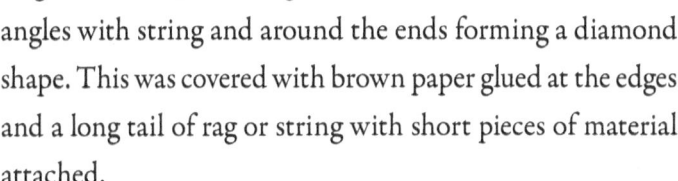 angles with string and around the ends forming a diamond shape. This was covered with brown paper glued at the edges and a long tail of rag or string with short pieces of material attached.

There was a 'knack' to flying a kite. Some children ran with their kites to get them up, but the best way was to stand with your back to the wind and slowly let the string out as it caught the wind. It was particularly popular with boys. Some even ventured into box kites. This was a box shape with no tail.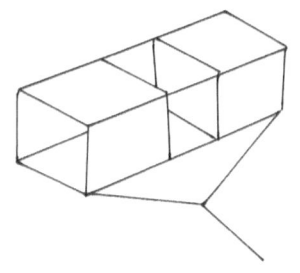

Most girls played with knucklebones. These were small anklebones from a sheep called Jacks. They were tossed in the air while kneeling or sitting on the ground, and caught on the back of the hand. I was surprised to read that this game went back to the ancient Romans and Greeks. I never played it as it was a girls' game. However, my cousin Joyce Attwood played it for hours and became quite skilled at catching them. Actually, girls still play Jacks today but the pieces are now multi-coloured plastic bone-shaped pieces and not real bones. Another girls' game was hopscotch. This was a game that involved drawing squares in the dirt, or with chalk on cement or bitumen, and hopping on one leg from one square to the next. Sometimes they drew a large helix and hopped around a circle.

In the 1930s, collecting cigarette cards was a craze and every kid had a collection. The cards came in a packet of cigarettes with pictures depicting a variety of subjects from film stars to the latest ocean liners, as well as cowboys and Indians. They are now collectors' items, but at the time every kid carried a bundle in his pocket and traded them with others. We also invented games with the cards. We would stand in a row, a set distance from a wall, and flick one card as close as possible to the wall. The winner, the closest, would then gather up all the cards and toss them into the air. Those that landed face upwards were his to keep.

Another memory of toys from the 1930s were cap guns. Most kids had a silver revolver to play 'Cowboys and Indians', inspired by the Saturday afternoon 'pictures'. I remember the distinctive smell of the caps exploding. 'Caps' were confetti-size red circles that came in a round box; I think it was a penny a box. They fitted into a slot in the revolver and a spring-loaded little hammer was drawn back with the thumb. When fired they gave a loud bang just like the cowboys shooting their guns in the movies. Every boy had one. These were followed by another type of toy pistol that took a long length of caps in a roll and they fitted into the firing mechanism and fired many loud bangs in succession.

Best of all were the water pistols. At first, they fired a single stream of water with a piston and cylinder action, then came the multi-shot versions. There were always two in a family for water pistol fights.

In the 1930s every kid knew how to fold a stiff piece of paper to make a paper aeroplane that flew quite well. I can still remember the folding procedure.

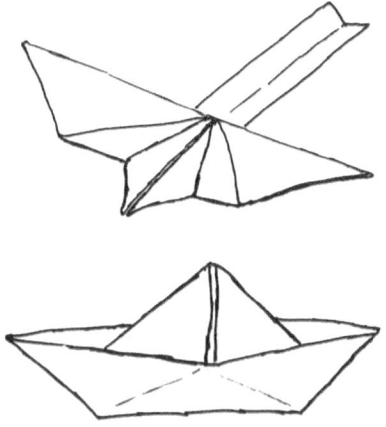

Likewise, we could all fold paper to make a paper boat.

Then there were tennis ball games. The most brutal was 'branding'. A group of about ten ran around in a confined area, and one person was 'in'. That kid had to pick a target and throw the ball to hit a runner, preferably on the buttocks. The victim retrieved the ball and chased someone else to deliver the same punishment. A quieter tennis ball game was just a contest of bouncing the ball with one hand until it was missed, and then scores were compared.

There were other games that involved bouncing a tennis ball against a wall and catching it. The girls dominated these games. They involved bouncing the ball against the wall, then turning completely around to catch it again.

One ball game that involved boys was 'five-stone'. This consisted of placing four stones at the corners of a square, about eighteen inches away from a wall, then placing the fifth stone in the centre. At about nine feet back, a line was drawn and the thrower had to bounce the ball from the square onto the wall and catch it. If it clipped the centre stone and the thrower still caught the ball, the score was fifty, but if it clipped one of the four at the corners of the square and the thrower still caught the ball, the score was one hundred. I played this game at recess in the playground; I didn't consider it a girls' game.

Skipping was always regarded as a girls' game, but sometimes boys joined in. There were many variations of skipping with one rope. There was slow skipping and there was 'pepper', which was turning the rope very quickly.

With a long rope, as many as eight or ten could all skip together, but if one person hit the rope, they dropped out until there was only one left. Actually, I have seen a line of girls skipping with two ropes going in different directions. I believe it was called double Dutch skipping. Girls had songs they sang while skipping that all seemed to end with 'pepper' until everyone was 'out'. I would say that in the 1930s, skipping was the dominant game for girls.

A quieter game for girls was cat's cradle. Girls would play for hours with a loop of string making various patterns. I could not see the sense of it, so I never played it at all.

Speaking of making things, I made a pom-pom in Second Class at primary school craft class. Firstly, we cut two circles of cardboard, the diameter of a cup. Then we positioned a two-shilling piece in the centre and cut out a hole from each piece. We had to provide a ball of coloured wool and wind smaller balls from it. These smaller balls were wound around the two pieces of cardboard held together, by passing the small ball of wool through the centre hole and winding wool around the two pieces of cardboard. This took many craft afternoons until it was hard to get any more wool through the central hole. Then the teacher forced the blade of a pair of scissors through the wool and between the two pieces of cardboard. She cut the wool all the way around and then tied a piece of string tightly between the two pieces of cardboard to hold all the wool together. She removed the two pieces of cardboard, and fluffed up the woollen ball. She then trimmed the uneven lengths to make a woollen sphere.

Some of the games we played in the 1930s need to be recorded for posterity. After lunch when the big boys were kicking a football, the younger ones played 'puss-in-the-corner' in the lunch shed. Four boys stood in each of the corners while a fifth boy in the middle was called puss. When he was not watching, two of the boys in the corners exchanged positions. If 'puss' was quick enough, he raced one of them for the corner position, then the one without a corner was 'puss'.

Another game we played mainly at birthday parties was

'blindman's bluff'. We always called it 'bluff' but research revealed that it was originally, 'blindman's buff' because the player who was blindfolded was buffeted by the other players. Rules vary, but our 'blindman' had to catch and name the person caught; if correct, then the person caught and named became the person blindfolded.

The most popular birthday party game was always 'postman's knock'. The American version originally gave each person at the party a number, even for girls and odd for boys. The nominated postman called out a number and had to kiss the person of that number. The Newcastle version was that the postman named the person and announced the number of letters he had for her. He consequently kissed her that many times. It was designed to break down shyness between boys and girls in the 1930s.

More of an activity than a game was swinging on swings. Dad made me a swing under the house at Queens Road. Because the land was sloping, the house was high at the back and I could explore among the piers that descended in size towards the front. My swing was about half way back and had a square seat, a bit over a foot square. Four thin ropes with knots under the seat at the four corners took the weight and it was attached to a floor bearer above. Before I had a little brother to play with, I spent a lot of time just contemplating on that little swing. There was always a rush to the swings in a park. I remember very high swings at Katoomba. They must have been twelve feet high. By standing and bending my knees and pushing, I could get them nearly horizontal. I loved swings!

Then there was Kotara Park. This was a new park in an outer suburb of Newcastle that was full of playground equipment. The Tighes Hill Sunday School organised Saturday afternoons out there. Most popular was a horizontal swinging board about nine feet long. It was held by four metal supports that allowed the board to be swung forward and backwards, remaining horizontal. It was propelled by two big kids with up to six squealing little kids holding the side supports.

Above all, games, besides being physical exercise, played a huge part in personality development. It encouraged getting on with fellow playmates as well as developing confidence and promoting organising ability. It was all part of 'growing up' in the 1930s.

CHAPTER 7

Holidays

Because Dad worked with the New South Wales Railways, he received two Privilege passes each year for himself and family to travel free to a nominated destination, and one Holiday pass to travel on any train, anywhere in New South Wales free for two weeks. Mum was a wizard at using them to the maximum advantage. We often had a long weekend in Sydney or long trips around New South Wales sleeping in the train by night. Once we slept on an overnight train, arriving at Moree in the morning, had a day swimming in the hot artesian baths and boarded another overnight train back to Newcastle. Not many kids would travel several hundred miles for a swim.

Our favourite holiday was a few days in Sydney staying at the People's Palace in Pitt Street. This was an accommodation place run by the Salvation Army. With 'no frills', it was basic and reasonably priced. Just to stay away from home was a novelty. The clean smell of newly ironed sheets, a new cake of soap, hot water coming out of a tap, deep baths and a dressing table with a Bible in one of the drawers were all new experiences for two little Newcastle boys. It may have been the cheapest accommodation in Sydney but it was absolute luxury for my brother and me. The elevators, the fire escapes, the tiled bathrooms, the smell of big pots of porridge cooking, the rattle of china plates, and butter in little rolls on a small plate were all eye-boggling. We looked at the views from our window; we looked at all the people. We were fascinated by all the new sounds and smells, and the clouds of steam in the bathroom and kitchen; it was all a new adventure.

We loved the People's Palace, but that was only the beginning. Next came trams that were a different shape to the Newcastle trams, followed by the ferry ride. On the ferry deck, we were overawed by the closeness of the bridge. There was no Sydney Opera House in those days; in fact, it was a tram shed. Seemingly dozens of tramlines all converged on a row of tram sheds, like a model train set. Lots of trams seemed to be all moving at the same time; some coming in and others going out. It was a hive of activity.

But the best part of the Manly ferry was going inside and looking down at the working engine. There was the smell of steam and hot oil and the sound of pistons thumping back and forth; everything to watch at once. The polished brass was gleaming. Huge pieces of machinery were spinning around. It was all unbelievable, and the size of everything was enormous. I am sure our mouths were wide open in wonderment; it was so fascinating.

Over the years we went to Manly and the Taronga Zoo several times and it was a thrill every time. Trips to the zoo were by tram, so we would enter from the top and walk downhill running from cage to cage. In those days the animals were enclosed in cages with iron bars, except for the monkeys. The monkey pit was always the most interesting; we watched it for a very long time.

Dad always carried the brown port containing our lunch, a teapot, a small square tablecloth, Nally Ware plates and picnic cutlery. He would take the teapot and go looking for a kiosk where he would get it filled with hot water for tea.

The family walking down the ramp at Sydney Central Railway Station

A highlight of a trip to the zoo was a ride on the elephant, which cost sixpence. We had to climb up steps to be sat in two rows back-to-back, and the elephant walked around a circular path. Some kids cried with fright but we loved it. Our trips to Taronga Zoo were always tiring but enjoyable.

We also liked the Sydney Royal Botanic Garden and had many visits there walking all the paths. The most adventurous of all our trips to Sydney was climbing a pylon of the Sydney Harbour Bridge right to the top to see the view of Sydney. There were no bridge climbs in those days.

The strangest of all places in Sydney was the Domain with all the speakers. At that time in the 1930s there would be over a thousand people in the Domain every Saturday afternoon. It was the place of 'free speech', and anyone who had something to say stood on a soapbox and said it. I can remember small groups and large groups standing all over the park. Most speeches were political or religious, and others were on the strangest topics, but someone always listened. We just walked from group to group to hear what they were saying.

In Sydney, Mum also took us to the art gallery, as well as to the Australian Museum where I was fascinated with the exhibits. Mum also took us to the Technological Museum in Harris Street. I remember pressing buttons and operating models of steam engines in glass cases. It was a little boy's delight, but best remembered was the model of the Strasbourg Clock. This was a huge model of the real one in France and visitors sat in rows of chairs and waited to see it strike on the hour. There was a series of events that took place; a rooster crowed, cherubs turned over a sand glass, a model of Jesus came out of a door and the twelve disciples walked around him, then the clock struck the hour. There were models of stars in their relative positions; all very technical, but absolutely fascinating.

One night while staying at the People's Palace, Dad and I went for a walk just to look at the city lights. It was a 'father and son' thing, strolling along slowly with hands behind our backs, looking at everything. Mum and Bruce stayed in the bedroom; both said that they were too tired for a walk. It was probably after a busy day. Going up the ramp to Central Station, I remember the city lights as well as seeing an old man selling combs. He was constantly shuffling and shaking. His speech was slurred. He held a tray full of men's combs with a strap over his shoulder and around his neck. Attached to his tray was a painting on a piece of cardboard of a war scene, with a cannon and lots of red and yellow cannon blasts radiating from a central point. There were Australian World War I 'tin hats' being blown into the air.

'What's the matter with him?' I remember asking my father.

Dad replied slowly and solemnly, 'Shell shock.'

I could see tears in Dad's eyes as he took two shillings from his leather purse and forced it into the man's hand. The man fumbled with the change but Dad waved him away. He offered Dad a comb and again Dad waved it away, so the man stuck it in Dad's top pocket. The man reminded him of his father and he became very emotional. That brown comb was stuck by its teeth in the cord that supported the little rectangular mirror that hung in the bathroom of the Tighes Hill house and later in the laundry of the Islington house for years. I wonder if Dad was reminded of the returned soldier with shell shock and also of his own father every time he used that comb? Sad memories.

We strolled through Central watching people walking in all directions. I was overawed with the huge neon signs. I remember a large bunch of purple grapes dripping into a wine glass. Moving neon signs were fairly new. There was a huge clock that hung from the roof that must have been at least six feet in diameter and was two-sided. Central was a meeting place. People said, 'I will meet you under the clock'. So, there were always groups of people waiting for friends under the clock. There was the cleaner who had a kerosene tin with a forty-five-degree lip at the front attached to a stick. He walked around Central with a broom in his other hand constantly sweeping up rubbish.

I was always spellbound with the big yellow board listing all the incoming and outgoing trains. There was always an exciting atmosphere at Sydney Central; it was the beating heart of Sydney. I remember the machine that pressed names on an aluminium strip. It was modern technology in the 1930s, but it would be very primitive now. It stood along the northern wall of the main station not far from the clock. It was enamelled cast-iron about three feet high and had a round dial on top with all the letters of the alphabet in a circle about a foot in diameter. It was coin-operated. Firstly, a coin was inserted. I think it was a penny, because other coins would not have been heavy enough, and besides, at the time weighing machines, as well as toilet doors, were operated with

Chapter 7 Holidays

a penny in the slot. It may have been more than one penny. The instructions were written clearly. A central arrow like the hand of a clock could be rotated to be opposite a letter, then it was pressed down firmly by a knob on the arrow. It was moved to the next letter and the process repeated until the name was spelled out. Finally, the knob was pressed at 'Completed' and an aluminium strip about half-an-inch wide and six inches long dropped out. Dad did it for me because strength was needed to press the knob downwards, and out came, 'RICHARD GRIMMOND' with a space each end.

Back home, Dad attached it to my schoolbag with bifurcated rivets. These were small brass rivets with two legs that were spread apart and hammered into the soft leather. I had my name on my school bag right up to the time Mum bought me a Globite port for high school. I was always reminded of that clever machine on Sydney Central Railway Station.

I will never forget my interesting holidays in Sydney while growing up in the 1930s.

Other holidays in the 1930s were our camping trips to Bulliac and Croudace Bay in our twelve-foot-square tent. Bulliac is a rural area with a railway station on the Gloucester River between Gloucester and Taree. We always went with the Anderson family. Arch Anderson was Dad's friend from the Honeysuckle Railway Workshops. He owned a Harley Davidson and sidecar, the same model as Dad's. The men would ride their Harley Davidsons from Newcastle with all the camping gear on the bikes and the wives and children would come by train using their railway passes. We had permission to camp on a farmer's property not far from the railway station and near the fast-flowing Gloucester River.

The Andersons had a tent with a ridgepole and had to chop down a couple of saplings before putting it up. Our square tent came with 'shop' posts with ferules to join two halves together. After putting up the tents and digging a trough around the perimeter with an axe for the rain, we all went gathering bracken fern. We filled the hessian mattresses with ferns and laid them on a piece of canvas inside the tent. We even fit the Harley inside the tent and Mum used the sidecar as a food cupboard through the sidecar door. We had a collapsible wooden table with detachable legs and fold-out stools. A Primus cooked our meals. A Primus was a kerosene-fired stove that was primed with methylated spirits. With our Nally Wear plates and aluminium cutlery we were very comfortable camping in the 1930s.

The men went shooting every day with their .22 rifles and the kids played by the river. We could swim in the still pools but the rapids were dangerous. When we were not swimming, the wide stretches of the river were still with a mirror-like surface.

It was here that Mr Anderson's son, also Arch Anderson, taught me to skip flat stones. In the 1930s every kid could skip stones. This entailed selecting a very flat stone from along the edge of the river. Then it was held in a very special way, between the forefinger and thumb with the flat sides horizontal. Before throwing the stone, the secret was to bend forward and concentrate on throwing the stone to hit the water on its flat side. This caused it to bounce or skip over the surface with several 'skips'. We had great pleasure seeing our stones skip over the surface up to fourteen times in a graceful arc before stopping and sinking in the other side of the river.

Another memory of Bulliac was crossing the rapids at its narrowest part on a log that had been flattened along the top edge with an adze or a saw. It was very scary seeing the white rapids below when the only hand-rail was a tight, single length of fencing wire. The wives and the children crossed the river every day to go up the hill on the other side of the river to get milk from a dairy farm. The farmer was feeding poddy calves with milk in a bucket and he showed us how to hold our fingers in the milk so the calves could suck them. It was a brand-new experience for city kids.

We camped at Bulliac two consecutive years, 1935 and 1936, and always in October for good weather. I have fond memories of Bulliac; I returned there as a teenager and canoed down the Gloucester River from Bulliac to Georges River many times in my Canadian canoe.

Our other family camping holidays were on the shore of Lake Macquarie at Croudace Bay, again with the Anderson family. The Andersons had a galvanised-iron 'weekender' on the shore of the lake and we joined them for Christmas holidays. Dad took all the camping gear in the Harley and Mr Anderson took our family in his Harley.

Dad pitched our tent on the grass at the edge of the lake next to the weekender. He always built a windbreak with

The two 1927 Harley Davidsons

small gum trees, held up with tent guy ropes for protection from the winds coming across Lake Macquarie from the south. The Andersons owned a rowing boat and prawning net so we went out on the lake fishing every day and prawning along the edge of the lake at night.

Mr Anderson's son was a little older than me. He had a galvanised-iron canoe. This was a crude homemade boat that was very common with kids in the 1930s who lived near water. It was made from a sheet of corrugated iron or flat iron bent to the shape of a boat. Mostly the corrugations were beaten flat before it was shaped into a boat. Firstly, a piece of wood about eighteen inches by a foot was shaped like the letter 'D' and turned sideways for the back and the iron was nailed to it. The front was nailed to a three-inch by one-inch vertical piece of wood for the bow. To make it waterproof, tar was melted in a jam tin and applied liberally front and back to fill the cracks.

Chapter 7 Holidays

In the 1930s, many roads in Newcastle were sprayed with tar before the blue metal or crushed stones were spread on them. It left areas of uncovered tar at the edges of the road. This was a little boy's delight. We used to pick up the soft tar and play with it like plasticine until our fingers were black. It was very hard to wash off. Apart from playing with the tar, there were often bubbles in the tar about two inches across that could be burst with a 'pop'. Sometimes the bubbles were filled with hot water on a sunny day. So, when little boys wanted tar, the edge of the road was a ready source. It could be melted in a jam tin and liberally applied to all the places in the canoe where water could get in. It looked a mess but it was effective.

Because the tin canoe was easily tipped and sunk, the 1930s kids were bright enough to only go in waist-deep water. These canoes were dangerous, but every second kid who lived near water had one.

One day when it was too cold for swimming, some children were throwing stones into the lake from Mr Anderson's jetty. A jetty was a homemade wharf about two-feet wide and about twenty-feet long and used for getting into the rowing boats without getting wet feet. One of the children throwing stones was my brother, who would have been about four at the time. It was just something to do to make a splash – throw the furthest or nearest to the post to which the boat was tied. Bruce must have been standing too close to the edge when he threw his stone. A gust of wind tipped him over the edge and he fell into the lake. Being a cold day, he was wearing a very thick jacket and this gave him buoyancy as he floated face downwards in the water. Being only eight and not yet able to swim, I feared that the water would be over my head, so I ran screaming down the jetty and into Mr Anderson's weekender where the mothers were sitting beside a fire, yelling that Bruce had fallen in the lake. Mrs Anderson was first out the door and ran into the water waist-deep fully clothed but Mum dashed along the jetty and jumped in and picked up Bruce and hugged him. With much drying of clothes around the fire, it was a very relieved group, after what might easily have been a tragedy.

Besides swimming and fishing, the children of both families also caught poddy mullets for the adults to use as bait. Poddy mullets were small mullets about four inches long. We caught them in a pickle bottle with a small piece of bread. A pickle bottle was ideal because it was just over an inch in diameter and about seven or eight inches long. The small fish swam in to eat the bread and could not turn around to get out. We had a string around the neck of the bottle with the other end tied to a stick on the jetty. It was good fun.

Catching large crabs was also very rewarding. Dad made a frame at work that consisted of an eighteen-inch diameter circle of quarter-inch diameter steel, with two half circles of the same steel welded to it and crossed at the top, forming a hemispherical frame. A friend gave Dad a bag of horsehair from brushing his horse's tail and our family sat for hours at nights before we went on holidays making little loops and tying them on every part of the frame. The object was for the loops to pull tighter when the crab was caught in them. Fish bait was hung in the centre, and a rope attached to a cork on the surface indicated its position. We would catch a crab every night, boil it in a kerosene tin and share it among the families. They were delicious. I have happy memories of camping at Croudace Bay. Camping was common in the 1930s; in fact, hundreds of tents belonging to the Maitland and Cessnock miners filled Bolton Point at Belmont and other sites around Lake Macquarie each Christmas.

Besides camping holidays, we went to Katoomba several times. We always stayed at places with bedrooms and a kitchen so Mum could prepare our own meals. This form of accommodation was the most popular at the time. I can remember going on walks and looking at waterfalls, especially at night with floodlights on them. They were spectacular to two little boys. We went on the steep Scenic Railway. Yes, it was operating back in the 1930s but didn't have the safety devices the present generation enjoys. It was just an open wooden truck with sloping seats and a long rope, but it was still scary to go down at such an angle.

One of my memories of Katoomba as a young boy was making mountain devils, which were face-shaped seed pods that grew in the bush around Katoomba. Children collected them, then using pipe cleaners bought from shops; they bent them into shapes that resembled people. The shop-made mountain devils always looked better and were for sale in the local shops. We probably saw them in the shops, then attempted to make our own.

Another unusual feature of the era were the rude postcards in the front windows of the newsagencies. As odd as it seems now, postcards with colourful drawings lined the windows along the bottom and down the sides. People were lined up reading them. They were all risqué. One that I can remember was of a housewife on her knees scrubbing the floor when a cat knocks the broom over and it strikes her bottom. The caption is, 'One loaf please, baker'. The inference being that she thought that the baker had hit her bottom with the broom. Apparently, that was the sense of humour for those times. I remember another one showing a couple being photographed between two short columns with containers on the top of each column that resembled a bedchamber pot. The caption was, 'Do you like the pose?', the inference being that the containers were 'poes', another name for chamber pots. People would burst out laughing and rush inside and buy the postcard, saying, 'I am going to send it to ... (so and so)'.

Train travelling in the 1930s was very different to today's train travel. Firstly, trains were pulled by steam engines, puffing and blowing smoke and steam.  There was no air-conditioning, so windows were open. This caused problems when the train entered a tunnel. The carriage filled with smoke and coughing passengers rushed to close the windows.

Also, when a cattle train passed going in the opposite direction or stood alongside us at a siding, there was another rush to close the windows because of the smell. Kids loved to look out of open windows but the cinders blew back from the engine and parents had to remove them from children's eyes with the corner of a white handkerchief. In most carriages, a large flat-bottomed bottle of water and two glasses were held in a bracket and everyone used the same glass for a drink of water. It wouldn't happen these days.

It would shock passengers today to see the ground and the sleepers passing under the toilet. All train carriage toilets were open. There was a notice saying, 'Please refrain from using the lavatory while the train is in the station'. How disgusting, but it was a reality in the 1930s.

We had several types of carriages. For long distance trains there was the box carriage. These were single compartments that held up to twelve people but there was no access to the rest of the train. There was entry to a toilet in the corner if one passenger stood and opened a door behind the seat.

There were also corridor carriages that had similar compartments, but a corridor gave access to the rest of the train with toilets at the end of the carriage. The compartments were beautifully made with Australian red cedar and red leather upholstery. They had luggage racks the full length of the seats and a row of black-and-white photographs of scenic New South Wales along the walls.

For heating in the older models, there was a huge metal container, over a yard long, filled with a liquid that contained caustic soda. It heated on agitation caused by the movement of the train and passengers pulled them from under the seats and put their feet on them for warmth. In some old carriages there was a brass spittoon recessed into the floor in the centre of the compartment. It was conical, about a foot in diameter, with a small hole in the centre for old men to spit into. Disgusting!

Carriage windows had wooden slats that could be pulled down to shade passengers from the sun. Because there was no cafeteria on trains in the 1930s, one delight was to arrive at a station that had a refreshment room. This was announced by a loud bell ringing as the train came into the station. The 'Ding! Ding! Ding!' brought everyone to the doors and as soon as the train stopped (sometimes a bit before) there was a mad rush to the Railway Refreshment Room (or RRR) for coffee and fruit cake. Seemingly the whole train load of passengers formed a stampede along the station and then struggled and pushed, many deep at the counter. Miraculously, everyone was served. Some drank it there and others took it back to the train. The deposit on the RRR china cup could be refunded at the next refreshment station. Perhaps it was because we were all tired in the middle of the night, but those cups of coffee and fruitcake were the best we had ever tasted and will live in my memory forever.

In the late 1930s, Mum booked a holiday to St Kilda in Melbourne, and we travelled down in the new *Spirit of Progress*. This was an ultra-modern, blue-and-gold train with a streamlined engine that we changed at Albury. Passengers had to transfer from one train to another; that is, from a four-feet-eight-and-a-half-inch gauge to a five-feet-three-inch rail gauge at the border. Compared with all the New South Wales trains we had been on, the *Spirit of Progress* was super modern. We were able to use Dad's railway pass from Sydney to Albury, but I think we had to pay extra to travel in Victoria; but it was worth it. We stayed in a little flat on the harbour shore at St Kilda and went for walks around Port Phillip Bay to Luna Park. We visited Captain Cook's cottage in Fitzroy Gardens and Mum organised a trip over MacRobertson's chocolate factory, long before it was taken over by Cadbury. Yes, we were given chocolate samples to eat.

We also visited the newly opened, impressive Shrine of Remembrance. It was a huge, white building in a large park, and designed so that a ray of sunshine shone on the Stone of Remembrance at exactly 11 am on the 11th of November each year.

I remember the cable trams; they were funny little things. The driver stood in the middle of the tram and worked a long lever that grabbed the cable or let it go. At a crossroad he would retain his momentum to coast across, then he would grab the cable again on the other side. We were fascinated with them.

In the late 1930s we had a radio, and every Friday night we listened to the Charlie Vaughn Show sponsored by Cox Brothers furniture   makers. Charlie was a comedian and he read out jokes that people had sent to the radio station. I think there may have been a contest. We never missed the show. So, knowing that we would be in Melbourne on a Friday night, Mum organised for us to be in the studio audience to see the show go to air. We met the celebrity and he shook our hands. It was a big deal for two young boys and we were very excited.

Looking back, I was lucky to have a mother who was a good organiser and made the best use of Dad's railway holiday passes.

Besides listening to Charlie Vaughn on Friday nights, we had other favourite radio shows that we listened to religiously. Of course, there was *Dad and Dave*, which everybody in Newcastle listened to. Other radio shows for kids were *The Search for the Golden Boomerang* and *Howie Wing*, about an aeroplane pilot, as well as *Yes, What?*, which was about a teacher and a class of naughty boys – we loved that one. The *Lux Play* was on Sunday nights as well as a serial called *The Woman in White*. I also remember *Martin's Corner*.

Besides half-a-dozen radio shows, there were also comics, such as *Mandrake*, *Tarzan*, *Ginger Meggs*, *Bib and Bub*, *Fatty Fin*, *Popeye and Olive Oyl* and many more. Then there were the continuing serials at the Saturday 'pictures' or movies. There was *Tom Mix*, *Hopalong Cassidy*, *Buck Rogers*, *The Green Hornet*, *Speed Gordon* and *Tailspin Tommy*, which was about a pilot of a light plane.

During the 1930s, the film industry was making giant steps forward. We were starting to be bored with silent Charlie Chaplin movies when we saw Al Jolson in the *Jazz Singer*. This was the first movie I ever saw with talking. About the same time, I remember seeing Walt Disney's first cartoon with Mickey Mouse in *Steamboat Willie*. When we went to

Chapter 7 Holidays

the pictures in the 1930s they began with a photograph of the King on the screen and the audience stood and sang 'God Save the King'. There were always two films, the main one and a second one, as well as newsreels, a cartoon and a travelogue, which was about another country and always ended with a sunset and the words ... 'as the sun sets, we say farewell to ...' There was often an *Our Gang* comedy. This was about a group of American kids getting into trouble. Every time a cartoon of *Our Gang* was titled on the screen, the kids in the front row would whistle and stamp their feet. It was the norm.

There was always an interval, when the lights came on and patrons went to the shop for lollies or chocolates, or went to the toilet. The toilets were always crowded and men and boys would be pushing and shoving, all facing a long urinal and urinating together.

Then there was the ubiquitous Peters ice-cream boy. He wore a uniform with a flat hat and held a large square tray filled with thrippeny cardboard cups of ice-cream with a little wooden spoon in each. He timed his loud call, 'Peters Ice!', for the instant the movie finished, and sometimes a second or two before it finished. He was always well patronised. Then there was the inevitable spilling of a packet of round orange Jaffas just after the lights went out, with noise of them falling down the wooden steps between the rows of seats and the whole theatre laughing. It happened every time.

Usually after interval, the smokers sent clouds of blue smoke upwards through the cone of light from the projector.

It was legal then. So, going to the pictures on Saturday nights in the 1930s was a ritual with a set pattern of accepted behaviour.

The Theatre Royal in Hunter Street had special shows for kids on Saturday mornings. I went to a few. One of their features was community singing. The words of the song would appear on the screen and a little bouncing ball followed the words so everyone sang in time. It was popular for a while. There was also a Theatre Royal Birthday Club and when your name was called out you went onto the stage and received a cream cake. Mum entered my name and when I received my cake the family went to Newcastle Beach and had it together. I also remember that the theatre had a special three-dimensional picture. This had to be viewed through cardboard glasses with one eye-piece red and the other blue cellophane. It was very effective; the audience ducked their heads when something appeared to be thrown from the screen.

In the mid to late 1930s, Charlie Chaplin was left behind and was replaced by Laurel and Hardy, then later Abbott and Costello. And, of course, the 1930s was the era of Shirley Temple and everyone just had to see her. My favourites at that time were Jeanette MacDonald and Nelson Eddy. They sang beautifully together, with the scenery of the Canadian Rockies behind them. Unforgettable memories!

So, without TV, going to the 'pictures' played a big part of our lives in the 1930s. In fact, I remember my first 'date' at the pictures when I was about eleven or twelve years old. I had mentioned to my school girlfriend, Lillian, that I was interested in the 3D picture that was advertised at the Theatre Royal and she had said that she was going to see it, so we made arrangements to meet at the theatre. We sat together holding hands tightly and pressing our sweaty cheeks together because we thought that was what people did on a date. I guess 'first dates' were no different in the 1930s to now, with youthful nerves and self-consciousness.

Speaking of going to the pictures, I remember going to The Strand, a theatre in Hunter Street, by myself when I was about thirteen. It must have been a predictable end, or people had seen it before, but many people were leaving early. When the lights came on, the theatre was half-empty and I noticed a fat wallet on the floor beside me. I picked it up but there was no one to ask who owned it because everyone near me had left, so I took it outside and handed it into the ticket office, saying that someone may return for it. It was obviously filled with notes. The girl thanked me for my honesty. When I told my parents, my mother said that I should have brought it home and tried to find the owner from information inside the wallet because there might have been a reward, but my father said that I had done the right thing being honest and handing it in. I often hoped that the ticket office girl was just as honest. I will never know.

CHAPTER 8
Washing Day

Monday was *always* washing day in Newcastle during the 1930s; it was a local cultural thing! Mum filled the copper with cold water from the tap over it. Then she set the fire in the bricked-in fireplace under it with newspaper and kindling. After the wood was burning, some lumps of coal would be placed on top of it, and before long the temperature of the water and the laundry would be rising. It was a good place to be on a winter's morning. Incidentally, a copper was an elongated semi-spherical tub about two feet in diameter and about eighteen inches deep, pressed from a single sheet of copper so it had no seams or joins and no drain to empty it. It had to be bailed out. It sat in a bricked-in fireplace about three feet square and two feet six inches high with a flat, horizontal concrete surface; there was a brick chimney in the far corner. The firebox had a little cast-iron door.

While the copper was heating, Mum stripped the beds, and gathered the towels and other things to be washed. They were all wrapped in a sheet and the big bundle was carried downstairs to the laundry and dumped on the floor. This would be the whole week's washing; there was only one washing day per week.

Some of the peculiarities of the 1930s should be recounted in order to appreciate the customs of the day. Firstly, only one sheet from each bed was washed. The upper sheet was transferred to the bottom for a second week and only the bottom sheets were washed. Next, a shirt was worn for the whole week; the thought is staggering these days, but it was perfectly normal for the 1930s. People in clerical positions, such as teachers and clerks, had detachable white collars held on with collar studs, so the collar was changed daily but not the shirt. My school clothes, including socks and singlet, were worn for the five days but we did change into 'old clothes' at the end of the school day to keep our school clothes clean. Sunday School clothes were separate; they were the 'best' clothes.

Back to the laundry. Firstly, the sheets were put directly into the copper, along with any items that did not have to be scrubbed. Those needing a scrub were tossed into a tub of cold water and scrubbed on the washboard. This was a framed, corrugated glass panel with two legs that went into the tub. Clothes were soaped with a piece of soap that sat in the wooden recess above the glass and scrubbed up and down against the glass ribs. A glass one was considered quite modern. Our auntie had a wooden one with horizontal ribs in the wood. The clothes would be scrubbed vigorously and rinsed frequently then rubbed again. This was the agitation process that removed the dirt. The clothes were then loaded

Chapter 8   Washing Day

into the steaming water in the copper and pushed below the surface with a well-worn copper pot stick. This was a piece of one-inch dowel rounded at both ends, probably an old broom handle, but it was bleached and softened with years of use in the boiling water.

A bar of homemade soap was pared into flakes with a rusty old knife that always sat near the copper chimney. This was long before soap powders came in cardboard boxes. The clothes and soap were poked below the surface of the bubbling water with the pot stick and a homemade wooden lid was placed on the copper while it boiled away for about an hour and filled the laundry with steam. After a few more pokes with the pot stick, the lid was put aside and the steaming-hot clothes were lifted from the copper with the pot stick and flopped into the adjacent tub of clean cold water. This would not have been an easy task because wet clothes are heavy to lift at that angle. When the tub was full, the clothes were rinsed of soap and fed up into the wringer that was turned by hand. They fell into another tub of clean water on the other side. After a second rinse, and another time through the wringer, they were tossed into the clothes box ready for the clothesline.

At this stage, the whites were separated out and they went through a tub of blue water. It was coloured blue with a knob of Reckitt's Blue. This was a little calico bag that always sat on the windowsill and it gave the whites extra whiteness.

Also, items were put aside that needed to be starched, such as collars of shirts, cuffs, doilies and serviettes. Starch came in a Silver Star brand cardboard box. A quantity was placed in an enamel dish and dissolved in boiling water. The items were dipped in it and excess squeezed out, then they were hung on the line to dry stiff.

With everything washed, blued and starched, they were taken to the clothesline in the clothes box. Mum preferred a box to a basket because she said the baskets didn't last, so Dad made her one with holes and rope handles. The clothesline was cleaned first from end to end with a damp cloth to remove Newcastle industrial soot, and then the clothes were pegged, using wooden 'dolly' pegs.

There must have been a quick look up and down the neighbouring backyards to see who won the prestigious competition of being the first out with the washing as the white sheets billowed in the wind.

As a kid I always felt sorry for Mum and dreamed of inventing a robot to do the work for her. I imagined a robot like the Tinman in *The Wizard of Oz*. Never did I dream that one day there would be a robot in the shape of a white cube with a row of buttons – the modern washing machine.

That hot soapy water in the copper couldn't be wasted, so it was bailed out with the aluminium dipper into a bucket, taken upstairs, and used by my mother to scrub the kitchen floor and back steps on her hands and knees. Housewives of the 1930s knew all about hard work.

On Monday night, before the socks were placed in their drawers, they were examined for holes or potatoes as we called them, and if found, put aside for darning.

Darning was a process of stretching the sock over a darner. This was a mushroom-shaped piece of polished wood that held the sock while threads of wool, the same colour as 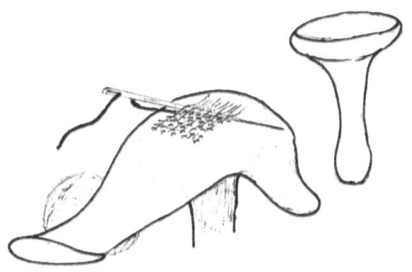 the sock, were sewn in parallel stitches over the hole with a darning needle. This was a special sewing needle with a large eye and a blunt point. Then stitches were sewn at right angles to the first lot in a weaving pattern.

Tuesday was always ironing day. This was done on the kitchen table on an old blanket and an old sheet. The irons were called Mrs Potts' irons because Mrs Potts, an American, invented the clothes irons with detachable wooden handles. There were always two or three irons in a set, which were heated on the fuel stove and removed with the detachable handle.

The irons were always wiped clean on a dampened cloth before use because a spot of soot on a white shirt would be disastrous. When the iron lost its heat, it was returned to the stove and another iron replaced it. Such was the process of ironing in the 1930s.

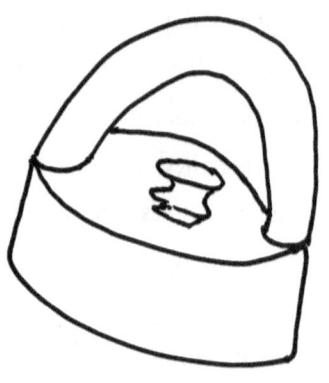

Friday was always cooking day. Newspaper was spread over the kitchen table and all the cooking dishes and equipment were spread around the table, including the very fat handwritten recipe book. Of course, there were no electric mixers in those days. I have seen Mum sit on a chair and hold a large bowl between her knees and stir vigorously with a large wooden spoon for ages. She would also pump up and down in a smaller bowl with a spring-like beater; but the most used beater of the 1930s was the hand-beater that was gripped by a handle on the top while turning a small handle at the side that drove two beaters.

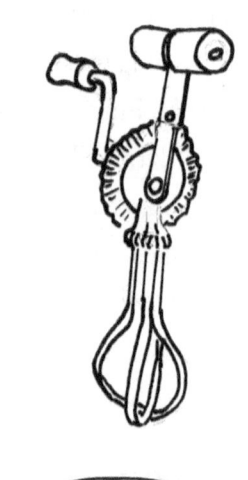

There was also a sieve for the flour that was hand-operated.

Anzac biscuits were always the favourite, but Mum made several types of biscuits as well as small cakes and scones. Her specialty was her sweet scones. These were scones that contained raisins and were always popular with the family, as were her fruit cakes and sponges. Cooking in a fuel stove meant keeping a constant heat supply and watching the fire. The room was always warm on cooking days, especially in the summer. Housewives in the 1930s were good cooks, as well as being good at housework, out of necessity.

CHAPTER 9

Shopping and other outings

My earliest memory of shopping was going to the butchers on the corner of Elizabeth and William Street in Tighes Hill. I would be given one shilling and one penny and had to ask for three pounds of chuck steak for a shilling and a sheep's head for a penny. The sheep's head was used to make soup.

I remember standing silently with others waiting, sometimes half an hour, for my turn to be served. I can still remember the smell of the sawdust and the Fly Tox. Fresh sawdust was spread an inch thick over the whole of the floor, probably to prevent slipping on blood and fat from the meat.

In the 1930s every butcher's shop had water trickling down the shop windows to prevent blowflies being seen by the public. It must have been done with a hose along the top with little holes every six inches. This formed a curtain-like pattern of loops of water all over the window. And there was always a row of fresh green parsley along the bottom of every butcher's shop window in Newcastle in the 1930s.

Whole carcasses of steers, sheep and pigs hung on hooks on a steel rail around the shop. The butcher wore a blue and white striped apron and appeared to be always busy. He held his sharp knife in a metal scabbard at his side and wielded a chopper on his chopping block. The chopping block was always a cross-section of a large tree that was hollowed on the top from continual use. He frequently scrubbed the surface with a wire brush to clean it.

When a customer placed an order, he sliced the cut from a carcass hanging around the wall and weighed it on the scales, wrapped it in white 'butcher's paper' then in newspaper. He got his newspaper from the general public. I made my pocket money by selling old newspaper to the butcher for a penny a pound. When the heap of old newspapers under the kitchen sofa started to get bumpy, I laid them on the floor in a tidy heap, rolled them into a bundle, tied them with string and took them to the butchers. I aimed at twenty

Chapter 9 Shopping and other outings

pounds, a convenient weight to carry, and I received one shilling and eight pence, or a penny a pound.

Dad always told me, if I saw a bolting horse on the way to the butchers, or even walking to school, that I should open the nearest front gate and go into a stranger's front yard. With all the horse and cart traffic, occasionally a horse bolted; that is, it raced away at full gallop pulling the bouncing cart, spilling the contents and usually tipping it over. This was caused by a fright, a car backfiring or even a sheet of newspaper blowing in the wind. It was not common but it did happen occasionally. I only ever saw one, and that was in the distance. It is certainly advice a father would not be giving to a son today, but it was part of the 1930s.

Our family weekly shopping was always at Mayfield on a Friday night. We went in the Harley and Dad and the boys sat with the Harley while Mum went from shop to shop to purchase groceries and green groceries. The outside brick wall of Miller's green-grocery shop was painted white and on a Friday night they projected silent movies of Charlie Chaplin to entertain the husbands while the wives shopped.

Shopping on Friday night was a social event, as lots of groups congregated and talked. That is simply not seen these days. More people appeared to know each other in the 1930s.

In the 1930s, every chemist shop had three huge round glass containers three feet high in the front window filled with different coloured liquids. Goodness knows why, but it was the symbol of a chemist. I remember also that in the chemist shop window in Mayfield, there was a small screen showing *Felix the Cat*.

Shopping at a grocer's shop was quite a ritual. The customer sat on a brightly painted stool advertising Arnott's biscuits, with her bag on her knee and a list in her hand, while the grocer dashed up and down the counter, even sliding sometimes. He snatched articles from the shelves behind him one at a time and placed them on the counter with a bang. If the customer wanted sugar, he scooped it from a bag of sugar and placed it in a brown paper bag and weighed it on the scales, carefully adding the contents of the scoop until the long thin needle of the scale was on zero. The sugar exactly balanced with the brass weights of one or two pounds on the scales.

If half a pound of butter was required, he gently indented two diagonal lines on the square pound of butter with a knife, then cut the butter in two halves with the cut going exactly through the intersection of the two indents to ensure a perfect division of halves. When biscuits were purchased, they were counted and placed into a brown paper bag, held by the two upper corners then swung around in the air to seal the bag by twisting the paper. When the list was completed, he produced the docket book and withdrew a sharp pencil from behind his ear. After inserting the all-important blue sheet of carbon paper under the first page, he started listing all the articles swiftly, in copperplate writing, and adding the prices. Nearly every item seemed to end in a halfpenny. He added up the list of figures and wrote down the total.

Then with a stern look on his face, as if to reinforce his honesty, he added it up a second time, tore out the docket and handed it to the customer.

With the money placed in the till with a ding-ding sound as the drawer opened and closed, the change was given. The grocer then reached for the wide roll of brown paper at the end of the counter and peeled off a long length. With one swift movement, he ripped it upwards against the straight edge and placed it on the counter. With the speed of a magician, he assembled all those odd-shaped purchases into a perfect cube and wrapped them up. He then reached above his head and grasped a piece of string from a coil hanging from the ceiling. Pulling down a length, he secured the parcel and tied a knot with a flourish. The next bit intrigued me as a kid. He wrapped the string around his thumb in a special way, then gave a quick jerk on the string and it snapped cleanly. I tried the same thing at home and nearly cut my thumb off. With the whole process completed, the groceries were handed over with smiles all around. Is it any wonder we invented the self-service supermarket?

The best part of Friday night shopping at Mayfield was getting a 'frost'. A frost was a type of ice-cream; it was orange and as big as a thrippeny ice-cream but only cost a penny. We boys had one each and even Mum and Dad had one, sometimes. On very rare occasions we had a milkshake. Would you believe that when they first came to Australia from America, they were four pence, or less than five cents in today's money?

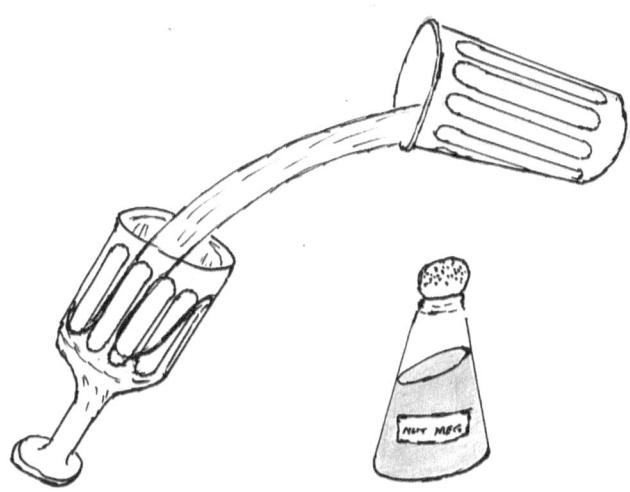

Milkshakes were milk and ice-cream mixed in an aluminium container. The milkshake girl would tip the milk from the container into the fluted glass in one swift movement with a graceful arc of milk in the air. In those days there was always a container of nutmeg on the counter to sprinkle nutmeg on top of the milkshake.

Another shopping expedition was visiting the big shops in Hunter Street. A trip to town was always exciting. I remember waiting in anticipation for the drinking fountain in Hunter Street, where the water came out of a lion's mouth. It was a huge sandstone monument on a corner, and a little boy's delight.

Also, a railway line for coal trucks crossed Hunter Street at forty-five degrees from a side street in the 1930s. When a coal train crossed the tram lines, it completely stopped all traffic until it passed! The coal train had a huge steam engine and a long row of full coal trucks. I can remember being held up for nearly half an hour often. Apparently, there was a coal mine somewhere past Merewether and this was its only access to the wharves.

Shopping 'in town' was mainly at Scott's or Winn's for material for sewing. Mum had a Singer sewing machine and made all my clothes and her own dresses, so we had to buy material. Like the grocer's shop this was also a ritual. It began with the pleasantries of 'What material is madam looking for?' Mum sat on a high cane-bottomed chair with her bag on her knee while the attendant, always a man in a suit, pulled down several bolts of material and flopped them onto the counter, unwinding a short length and holding it out with his hand. This would go on until there was an untidy pile along the wide counter. After the decision was made, the tense mood seemed to change to one of relief as the salesman measured out yard after yard on the brass rule along the edge of the shop counter. Holding the exact position firmly with his forefinger and thumb, the salesman reached for a large pair of scissors and made a small cut exactly where he held his thumb. Then with the speed and grace of an ice skater, the scissors zoomed across the material, much to the amazement of a little boy. The material was gently folded, and like the grocer, he peeled off a length of brown paper from the roll at the end of the counter and tore it against a straightedge. He wrapped the parcel and tied it with string. Then out came the docket book, the ubiquitous sheet of blue carbon paper, the flourish of copperplate writing, and the amount of money added. The top copy was torn out and presented to the customer. There was a fumble in the purse and a note was produced and handed over. Next was the interesting bit. The salesman reached above his head and unscrewed a wooden container about the size of a can of beans. He placed Mum's money inside, clipped the docket in a spring clip beneath it, reached up again, and screwed the container into a socket. He then pulled hard on a cord that stretched a rubber slingshot to its maximum length. At this point, it released the container and it sped along a wire on two little wheels at lightning speed, emitting a screeching sound that faded into the distance as it travelled 'somewhere' up near the ceiling. By this time, I was open-mouthed with wide eyes in wonderment as the missile streaked along the wire. After a pause, the container sedately rolled down the wire under gravity and stopped with a bump above the salesman's head. He unscrewed the container and handed Mum the change.

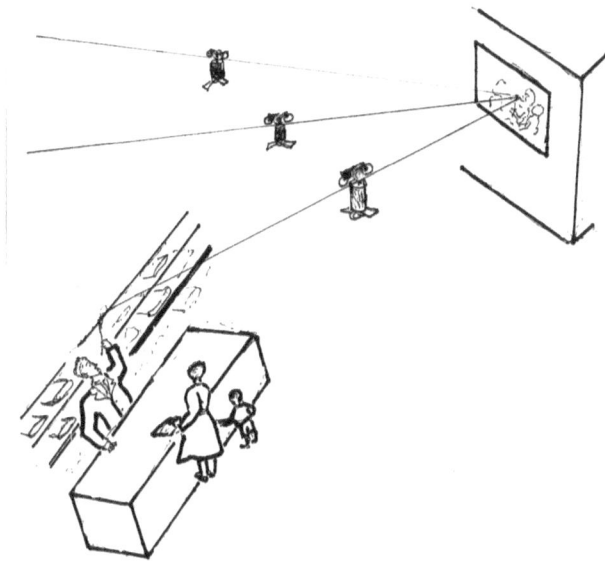

Chapter 9   Shopping and other outings

Like a metal spider web, lots of wires radiated from the office window and containers were going up and down all over the shop, much to my fascination.

There was another system that involved big black spheres like lawn bowls that ran around slatted troughs and turned corners on their way to the head office. I think these were at the Frederick Ash building, the hardware store in Hunter Street. These spheres also unscrewed and the salesman put the money and docket inside. They were raised up to a track by pulling on a rope, and gravity took them along. They returned on a higher track.

In the late 1930s, Winn's became modernised by using a suction system that replaced the overhead wires. The salesman inserted a slightly smaller round container with the customer's money and docket inside into a white tube that sucked it in with an audible inhalation. It could be heard travelling through the long white tubes that were around the walls of the shop to 'somewhere' in the distance. After a pause it returned and was spat out with a burp.

Then there were the elevators, or 'lifts' as we called them. These were usually operated by a one-armed or one-legged man who opened and closed the door for you. He announced all the items sold on the approaching floor with a loud, very fast, almost 'singing', voice, again much to my amusement. I giggled at the announcement of 'ladies underwear', a subject never mentioned in public. It was all part of shopping in the 1930s.

In the late 1930s when I was much older, I remember going to the Arnott's biscuit factory in Union Street, Cooks

Hill, on a Thursday morning to buy broken biscuits for sixpence a scoop. A scoop was more than half a pillowslip full. On Thursday mornings from 7 am, all over Newcastle there was a steady stream of bike riders with a bulging white pillowslip between the handle-bars of their bikes. Apparently broken in the manufacturing process, there were mountains of broken biscuits and they were very popular at the time. Bought biscuits were a luxury in the average home in the 1930s, so they were in high demand.

From shopping at Mayfield on a Friday night, to special trips to Scott's and Winn's, or going to the butchers; it was all one big adventure for a little kid growing up in Newcastle in the 1930s.

Going to Newcastle Beach in the 1930s was a big part of our lives. As I previously mentioned, I used to go to Newcastle Beach with Mr Mabbit and Dad on a Saturday morning when I was very young and we also went to surf carnivals as a family. I remember Newcastle lifesavers competing with the Sydney clubs on Newcastle Beach and the spectacular marches with all the colourful swimming costumes.

I remember the surf rescue races where four men carried the surf reel, and a line of lifesavers reeled out the thin rope over their heads in unison. Then they pulled the 'patient' in to the beach and performed resuscitation by straddling him on their knees; all very different to today's procedures.

Chapter 9   Shopping and other outings

Kids playing in the sand probably has not changed. The first instinct is to build a sand castle. It is not long before they work out that the tide comes in slowly and after a while the waves are going further up the beach, so it becomes a challenge to build a castle that resists the onslaught of the watery enemy for as long as possible. We used to build a high castle with a wall around it and a moat to take the water, but the sea always won and destroyed the fortress.

Then there was building the racing car. We needed help for this one. We sat down with feet forward while another kid covered our legs until we were waist-deep in sand in a racing car, complete with a sand steering wheel. It wouldn't be a trip to the beach without a racing car. So, playing in the sand was an experience of invention and initiative that was a challenge to active minds, and kept us occupied for hours.

Sunburn was ever-present. We learned very early to cover up. I had an old blue shirt that I wore under my swimming costume. It would get wet and stick to me, but it was better than sunburn.

Incidentally, in the 1930s our swimming costumes were made of heavy woollen material, with shoulder straps and a thick front skirt. Mum had sleeves in her costume.

Besides making sand castles, we loved exploring the rock pools and were intrigued with the little fish and anemones that closed up when touched. I suppose kids are exactly the same today.

I remember the black-and-white rubber surfoplanes for hire at sixpence a half hour. These were inflatable rectangles

Mum in swimming costume

about a yard by half a yard with a rubber handle on each side. Young fellows would catch waves with them. Occasionally, one would get away and the whole beach would watch it disappear over the horizon.

The Saturday afternoon atmosphere along Newcastle Beach in the 1930s was probably not unlike an English pier. Men and ladies 'promenaded' along the walkway dressed in suits and long dresses, eating ice-creams. There was a carnival atmosphere with a few tents, including one where a photographer would take your photograph using a plate camera on a tripod and with a black cloth over his head.

Chapter 9   Shopping and other outings

There was a fellow in another tent with a suspended weighing machine that you sat in. He would guess your weight and if he was wrong by more than a certain number of pounds, it was free, otherwise the customer paid.

Before I leave the beach, I must tell you about the board riders. Surfboarding was in its infancy, having been recently invented, and boards were literally boards of wood. I remember seeing the surfers using two-inch-thick planks of Oregon that were nine feet long and about a foot wide. They appeared very heavy by the way they carried them, but once in the water they could catch a wave and come in standing on them. Occasionally, they would ride a wave on their board standing on their heads. The whole beach would clap.

Little kids used to paddle with their clothes on along the southern end of the beach. My English grandfather would roll up his trousers above his knees and hold the hands of his two grandchildren, who were also fully clothed; my cousin with her dress tucked into her bloomers, or in my case, with pants rolled up showing the white lining. He would hold our hands and jump the small waves. I am sure that it was 'an English thing'.

I must tell you about the entertainment on the sand. Enterprising men made a razzle-dazzle and charged kids a penny a ride. A razzle-dazzle was a circular seat facing inwards, about twelve feet in diameter and suspended by metal supports from a central post dug into the sand. It was pushed around by man-power and it was deliberately swung high and low to entertain the squealing kids. I think the council banned them after there were a few broken arms when kids fell off.

Perhaps inspired by the razzle-dazzle men, I have seen petrol-driven swinging chairs held by chains on the southern end of Newcastle Beach. It was scary seeing people swung out nearly horizontally over the sea.

I also remember Scripture teachers who set up an easel and a roll of religious pictures on the Newcastle Beach and gave an improvised Sunday School lesson to anyone who wanted to watch.

But the best part of going to the Newcastle beach for a kid in the 1930s was having Saturday night tea with cousins and aunties at the picnic tables at the southern end of the beach. This continued for many years. I can remember that there was a long building with a kiosk in the centre. There were about twenty tables each side of the kiosk, as well as a lot of tables in the old stone buildings adjacent, and they were all occupied. When the shadows were lengthening, the tablecloths came out and the ladies started slicing tomatoes.

Chapter 9 Shopping and other outings

This seemed to be the most essential part of a family picnic. Meanwhile, all the dads started walking towards the kiosk with teapot in hand to get hot water for sixpence. They would often meet someone they knew on the way. With sand on our legs, we all packed around the table and had tea with the waves quite close. It was a child's delight. I loved Saturday tea at Newcastle Beach.

Besides going to the beach, we had many weekend picnics with the Harley. The 1930s was an era of family outings with the tablecloth on the grass and the whole family sitting around it. We usually put down a travelling blanket or a piece of canvas, particularly if the ground was damp. Sometimes it was sandwiches and other times it was a salad, but never a barbecue; barbecues didn't become popular until much later.

It was not unusual to see many families dotted over a popular spot. There were two distinct periods; the 'boil the billy' period, and the 'Thermos flask' period. In the early 1930s, a family picnic would always boil the billy, and it was the men's job to collect wood and make a fire to boil the water for the tea, but later the Thermos flask saved a lot of work.

Roadside meals were so popular that government departments constructed fireplaces along all highways, and they were well used in the 1930s and 1940s. There are still a few left but we have now entered the era of coffee stops and prepared meals. A car stopping by the side of the road reminds me of flat tyres. In the 'old days' we would *always* see someone changing a tyre by the side of the road. Often other motorists would stop and assist. These days, with mobile phones, quick

NRMA response times and better-quality tyres, something that used to be common is now rare.

On one of our weekend picnics in the Harley, we visited Karuah, a small village on the northern shore of Port Stephens, about forty miles north of Newcastle. Mum met an old school friend. We had selected a picnic table with a pleasant water view, and on this particular day, when the family on the next table exchanged smiles and pleasantries, Mum asked the mother, 'Are you Alice Rodgers?'

Then there was much hugging and laughing as two old school friends from Teralba School recognised each other after years of family life since their last meeting. It was not long before life stories were exchanged and 'Auntie Al', as my brother and I were to know her, told us that she was living on a dairy farm at Twelve Mile Creek, about ten miles back along the Newcastle Road. She had two boys about the same age as me and my brother, all between seven and twelve. Naturally, we visited their farm on our way back home and a firm friendship was renewed. It was like another auntie, uncle and cousins, and our families remained very close for years.

I mention this family because farm life was another aspect of the Depression of the 1930s. Uncle Alf had about fifty acres, half-cleared and half-timbered, on which he ran thirty cows and a few pigs. His only regular income was from his cream, and that was five pounds per month, so they had to be self-dependent. Our families became very close and we visited them many times, often staying overnight.

Chapter 9   Shopping and other outings

Their day began while the frost was still on the ground and thirty cows were hand-milked. The head bails were all made with bush timber and a pole held the cow's head over a box of feed with a wooden pin in a hole. The milking stool was a small cylinder cut from a tree and the bucket was held between the knees of the person milking the cow. For 'city kids' like my brother and me, it was another new experience and an exciting adventure. At times we were shocked by things the farm boys did. As they were always in bare feet it must have been extremely cold in the frost so they would stand in freshly dropped cow manure to warm their feet.

I remember how horrified my brother and I were at witnessing the castration of the pigs, much to the amusement of the 'farm kids', so it was an education for us. Everyone in the family milked the cows, as well as the visitors, and the buckets were emptied into the separator. The separator seemed to be governed by lots of regulations. After it was used, every piece was washed in hot water and treated with the utmost of respect in its little fly-proof room. Turning the separator handle was hard work; everyone took their turn. It was magical to see yellowish cream pouring steadily out of one stainless steel pipe and bluish skim milk from the other.

When the milking was finished and the cream can filled, the farm horse, Biddy, was harnessed and attached to a slide. This was a Y-shaped branch from a tree, with a few flat pieces of wood nailed to it to form a platform on which the can of cream stood. This was harnessed to the horse and easily slid over the wet grass to take the can of cream to the front gate, from where it was picked up by the cream lorry at a precise time and taken to the factory at Raymond Terrace early in the morning.

With the cream delivered to the front gate on time, the family was able to relax and go back to the house for breakfast; this was always porridge, followed by eggs. There were always plenty of eggs because Auntie Al had many laying fowls. She let them out of their pen in the morning to peck around the house yard. Right on dusk she called them while shaking an enamel cup of wheat and they all went into their yard to get a couple of cups of wheat, and she could lock them up to be safe from foxes during the night.

I remember that one farm chore that intrigued me was cutting the feed for the cattle. Uncle Alf had a paddock near the house growing a crop he called sorghum. This was given to the cattle while they were being milked. He harvested it using a large scythe, like Father Time. His skill with this tool fascinated me. Firstly, he sharpened the blade with a stone that was about a foot long, cylindrical, and tapered at each end. He kept a constant angle and sharpened the blade in one continuous sweep after another until he was satisfied. He then swayed his body, keeping the blade just a couple of inches above the ground until he had a heap of mown hay. This he placed on a piece of hessian about nine feet square, then, holding the diagonal corners, hoisted it over his shoulder and carried it up to the milking sheds. He then put it through a chaff-cutter. This was a hand-operated piece of machinery that chopped the sorghum into short lengths. One of the boys turned the handle while Uncle Alf fed the greenery into a chute. Many farmers have lost fingers with this machine, so it was treated with respect. The cut chaff was stored in a half tank to be used next morning in the feed boxes for the cows.

While this was happening, Auntie Al had washed every part of the separator with hot water as per regulations. Uncle Alf then carried the kerosene tins with wire handles filled with the separated skim milk down to the pigsty and emptied them into the hollowed logs that had been made into troughs.

The family morning face wash was in an aluminium dish that sat permanently under the house tank tap. Because of water shortages, the whole family, including visitors, used the one dish of water that was carefully emptied into the pot plants after the last one. We learnt to be conscious of how precious water was in the country.

Another shock to city boys was the country lavatory. We were accustomed to flushing toilets at Newcastle and we had experienced pans at our auntie's place at Blackalls, but the Twelve Mile Creek lavatory was a hole in the ground about two feet square and six feet deep. When it was full, another hole was dug near it. The dirt from one hole filled the other hole, while the seat and wooden structure was placed on planks over the new hole. That was life on the land in the 1930s.

So close was our friendship with our new Auntie Al and Uncle Alf that when I was about twelve years old, I decided to ride my bike the twenty-eight miles from Islington to Twelve Mile Creek; I often went up for the weekend following the first trip. The first time was hard but it became easier with experience. In fact, I often took mates from school with me over the years. Of course, there were no bridges over the Hunter River at that time and I had to cross on the Hexham Punt, a huge vehicular ferry that held about twenty cars. I remember one time that I rode my bike up just before Christmas and it was a good year for Christmas bells, which are drooping bell-shaped flowers. Auntie Al had several bunches in vases in the house.

'Would you like to take a bunch home for your mum?' asked Uncle Alf. We set off on a big hike through the property picking Christmas bells. When he had a huge bunch, he put two small potatoes in the bottom corners of a sugar bag and tied a rope around them, making a haversack with rope straps. It was uncomfortable but it worked. By the time I rode the twenty-eight miles to Islington, the thin rope had made grooves in my shoulders that were most painful, but my mother appreciated the big bunch of colourful flowers. As it was illegal to pick them at that time, Uncle Alf gave me a note saying that they were picked on private property. That was one ride I will not forget.

Beside the farm equipment of cow head bails for hand milking, blocks of wood for stools, the hand-operated milk separator, the horse-drawn slide to carry the cream can, as well as the scythe, the chaff-cutter, the primitive toilet, and fuel stove, there were also kerosene lamps for lighting and only tank water; all necessary for life on the land in the 1930s.

Chapter 9 Shopping and other outings

Apart from family picnics at the weekends, we often visited my mother's relations at Charlestown. My grandmother on my mother's side lived in Charlestown, which was an outer Newcastle suburb just past Adamstown on the Sydney Road. There were coal mines still operating just out of Charlestown and my grandmother's brother, who we called Uncle Harry, looked after the pit ponies that pulled the trucks of coal underground. He kept them in a yard behind his house and when we visited him, we always went 'down the back' to pat the horses that were resting at weekends.

I particularly remember coming home from Charlestown after dark and seeing the lights of Newcastle from Adamstown Heights. For two little boys it was absolutely magical seeing the millions of little lights over the whole of Newcastle. We were always excited and called it 'fairyland', a permanent memory of childhood.

So, with our camping trips to Bulliac and Croudace Bay, as well as weekend family picnics and visits to relations, along with shopping expeditions and Saturdays at Newcastle Beach, we certainly enjoyed our Harley Davidson to the fullest. While we could see hardship all around us caused by the Depression, we were thankful that our dad had a permanent government job and that our mum was a good money manager with so little income.

CHAPTER 10

Our Identity Found

In 1901 we took our first step to be independent of England, but in 1914 Australia felt compelled to help England in World War I. After the war, in the 1920s, Australia 'let its hair down', 'kicked up its heels' and 'made merry', if I can mix my metaphors, relieved that the war was over, and tried to take on its own image. Girls had shorter dresses, smoked, drank alcoholic drinks and even bathed at the beach. Public perception of morals was more liberal, if I can put it nicely. We were striving for our own identity when the Depression of the 1930s united us as a nation, because we were all 'in the same boat'. We then found our own identity. This is evident in the evolving way that we expressed ourselves. We developed words and expression that were typically Australian and this made us different to the rest of the world.

Some words that are uniquely Australian are: 'G'day' (to say hello), 'bloke' for a man and 'sheila' for a young female; then comes 'bludger', meaning someone who does not do his fair share of the work; 'brolly' for umbrella, 'garbo' for the garbage man, 'brickie' for a bricklayer, 'smoko' for time off for a cigarette, 'arvo' for afternoon, 'a bogan' for an unsophisticated person, 'banana bender' is a Queenslander, 'crook' is feeling unwell, 'chunder' is to vomit, 'drongo' is a stupid or incompetent person, a 'dunny' is a toilet, and 'galah' is a person who does foolish things. To 'shout for someone' is to pay for a drink. To 'have a sickie' is to have a day off work because of sickness or pretend to be sick. Don't you just love them? To say you are 'buggered' means you are out of energy, 'to spit the dummy' means that you have become very annoyed. 'Fair dinkum' means something is genuine. A 'hankie' is a handkerchief or a 'snot rag' in cruder circles. 'Crikey' is an expression of surprise, probably a euphemism for 'Christ'.

Not only did Australians invent their own list of new words, mainly in the 1930s, they also threw in many phrases, expressions and sayings, such as 'beyond the black stump', meaning 'somewhere a long way away'. Around this time, Australians also borrowed many phrases from the English.

I remember the word 'furphy' meant gossip or an improbable story, which had its origins in the trenches of World War I. The watercarts that moved amongst the troops at the front line were made by the Furphy iron foundry in Shepparton in Victoria and had the company name on them. Many of the stories, picked up while getting a drink of water at the Furphy, turned out to be not true, so they were called 'furphies'.

My grandmother used to say, 'If there is enough blue in the sky to patch a sailor's pants, then it will be clear tomorrow.' It sounds silly now, but in the 1930s these expressions seemed to be there all the time. Things were 'the bees' knees', or 'not my cup of tea'.

Then there were family expressions that are never used now, like saying 'spill sugar for joy', when someone accidentally spills sugar, or throwing a pinch of salt over the shoulder for luck. I remember kids would never 'step on a crack', that is the line joining two sections of the concrete in a path. It was bad luck. What nonsense, but kids were superstitious in the 1930s. If my cousins or my brother and I saw a white horse, we kept our fingers crossed until we saw a dog, and could make a wish. Why on earth? It was just the custom of the day. And, of course, we would also 'make a wish' when we saw a falling star.

Speaking of wishes, there was always a fight for the wishbone from the Christmas chicken dinner. Two people held it with their little fingers, each closing their eyes and making a wish. Then both pulled until the bone broke. The person who held the larger piece of bone was the winner, and his or her wish would be granted. All these old customs need to be recorded for posterity. Then there was the excitement when a black cat crossed our path. That was a sign of good luck.

With all these old-fashioned sayings and expressions, as well as our slang, Australia found a character that made us truly unique, and we created our very own identity in the 1930s, that still remains today.

While Australia was starting to stand on its own feet, the rest of the world was going through changes in the 1930s. On one hand, the League of Nations was trying to get off the ground as war clouds were forming at the same time with a dictator in Germany named Adolf Hitler rising to power.

I remember reading about the League of Nations in the school magazine. It showed a picture of a big, white building in Geneva, Switzerland, where nations would settle their differences by negotiation. It sounded idealistic because as the rules were being made, the sound of gunfire was being heard at the same time when Japan invaded Manchuria in 1931 to obtain fuel for its developing industries. Then in 1935, Italy invaded Abyssinia. Again, I can remember school pupils talking about it in the playground and discussing whether it would turn into a world war like our parents had experienced.

We could see in the newsreels at the pictures that Germany was amassing vast armies. It all seemed so contradictory to the objectives of the League of Nations. Even as kids we were patently aware of that.

But there were highlights of the 1930s to counter the bad news. We welcomed the biggest ship ever built, the *Queen Mary*. This caused massive excitement in an unsettled world. It was in all the papers and movie newsreels, as well as on kids' cigarette cards. The world gasped at the size and marvelled that we lived in such a progressive age. In 1935, every schoolboy knew the name 'Malcolm Campbell' and his famous 'Bluebird' racing car, in which he broke world speed records. In 1935 he passed 300 miles per hour and we had pictures of him on our cigarette cards. Then in 1937, George Eyston, broke Malcolm Campbell's record with 357 miles per hour. They were exciting times for schoolboys.

Chapter 10 Our Identity Found

Even without television, we were aware of what was happening at the 1936 Olympic Games. They were well covered at theatre newsreels, as well as in the daily papers. We knew that Adolf Hitler had banned Jews, as well as coloured athletes, from competing in the German Olympic team. He actually expressed his opinion of white supremacy publicly and was obviously upset when Jesse Owens, an African American, won gold medals in the 100 metres and 200 metres races, the long jump, as well as a medal for the relay race.

In 1937, when the Hindenburg airship caught fire on docking in America with many lives lost, it was well-documented on film and we saw horrific photographs in the paper. It shocked the world and put an end to air travel for quite a while.

In 1935, an unusual event happened in Newcastle; at least I thought so. At that time, we were aware of the farthing coin, a quarter of a penny. It occasionally turned up in the small change as a curiosity, but it was not frequently used.

Then in 1935, I remember that Winn's, the big merchandise store in Hunter Street, suddenly advertised that the price of all their materials ended in one farthing or three farthings per yard. Even if the multiple yards ended in a round figure, they still gave a farthing in change. Apparently, they had an arrangement with the Royal Australian Mint to distribute the newly minted farthing coins. It was obviously an advertising exercise for Winn's and at the same time drawing attention to the fact that the Mint still made farthing coins. For the record, farthings ceased to be legal tender in Australia on 31 December 1960.

CHAPTER 11
Winding up the 1930s

When my family moved from Tighes Hill to our new house in Islington in 1937, we left behind the early 1930s and entered a new era of the late 1930s. A new gas stove with a side oven replaced the old fuel stove, a gas copper replaced the old laundry bricked-in copper, and an electric wringer replaced the hand wringer. We even had a bath heater. Mum had an electric iron now and we purchased a newly introduced gas refrigerator that Edward Hallstrom was making. And we actually had an indoor toilet. We even had a toilet-roll holder, so for the first time the family had toilet paper, although I will admit that when Mum bought apples wrapped in tissue paper, the tissue was placed in an old basket in the toilet and used as toilet paper until they were all gone. Mum was always 'saving'.

So, the late 1930s saw vast improvements in lifestyles. It was the turning point when Newcastle, and I suppose other towns as well, entered a new age. We even had whole lettuce leaves on our salads, shredded lettuce had also been left behind in the early 1930s. We had fly-screens on windows and flies were not the problem that they had been in the past.

Also, when we moved to Islington, Mum bought a Fowlers Vacola bottling outfit. This was a special drum that was heated on the stove and had its own thermometer permanently sitting in a slot. Mum had a ball. She sent away for cases of fruit and soon we had cupboards stacked with jars of peaches, pears, plums and pineapples. We had a Vacola dessert with every Sunday dinner. Mum had quite a long list of dishes that she made as well. Among them were stewed fruit, apple pies, banana custard, flummery, lemon sago, junket, jelly, and, of course, fruit salad.

About this time in the late 1930s when we moved into the new house, there was a craze all over Newcastle for making homemade ginger beer. All my aunties and our other friends were exchanging recipes and plants. Bottles were collected, the 'plant' was 'fed' for a certain period, and then the bottles were filled. We heard of disasters when bottles exploded in the middle of the night, but it was all part of the excitement. Again, it was an era that we passed through in the 1930s.

Dad was busy with the new house. There were lawns to be laid, paths to make and gardens to dig. The new block was very long; in fact, there were two houses along the northern fence and our block opened into a lane off Ivy Street, so we had a back entry.

Chapter 11 Winding up the 1930s

Mum had asked the builder, Mr Reynolds, to make us a shed for the Harley. After some haggling, the price was twenty pounds extra. Imagine a garage for twenty pounds. There was also a haggle over cement paths. Mum said that she expected paths to be included with a new house so a compromise was reached and the builder included a concrete path from the front gate to the north-western corner of the house. Dad would have to do the rest. I was nine, almost ten, so I was at an age when I could help. I remember 'a mate from work' dropping a couple of bags of Kikuyu over the front fence. This was a new grass that had just been introduced from South Africa. It was very popular when it first arrived, but people later discovered how 'invasive' it became. Dad and I raked the whole yard flat. The soil was soft and sandy. The two adjoining blocks had previously been a yard for horses, with stables along the back, so the whole block was well trampled and rich in horse manure. The stables had a sandstone floor, so Dad had plenty of stone for garden edging. After the yard was levelled, we broke the cuttings into short lengths and half buried them at intervals over the lawn and watered them well. The new grass grew very quickly.

Next came the paths. Dad was experienced at mixing because he had mixed plaster by hand at Crockett's plaster works. He always started making a big hill with a hollow in the centre, like a volcano, which he filled with water. Then he kept shifting the outside into the centre and mixing at the same time. Dad always stuck to the 1:2:3 proportions: that was one part cement, two parts sand and three parts aggregate. We mixed it on the new garage floor and carried it in buckets to the path. He used three-inch by one-inch hardwood formwork for the path and packed it with broken bricks and stone before adding the wet cement. He vigorously screeded it, using the formwork as a guide. Then he mixed a special batch of wet cement without aggregate, for 'top dressing' and finished it with a big trowel.

We laid concrete paths along the back of the house to the backdoor steps, as well as alongside the shed, to the clothesline and one at forty-five degrees across to the garage door. We were well-pleased with our efforts.

Dad then made gardens. He dug one completely around the front lawn and made the garden edge with the sandstone blocks from the horse stable floor along the back fence. Next there were gardens the full length of the fences each side, with a large patch near the back gate for vegetables. The first crop to go in was potatoes in a large patch twelve feet by twelve feet. These were 'hilled' in preparation for easy digging when we had a crop. Next was rhubarb, and as soon as they started to grow up, a bottomless kerosene tin was placed over them to encourage them to grow taller. Dad planted beans and chokos, as well as tomatoes, lettuce, beetroot and onions. It was not long before Mum was completely independent of the greengrocers.

Then Dad concentrated on flowers. He grew dahlias. A 'fellow at work' was shifting house or going on holidays, so for some reason he gave all his dahlia bulbs to Dad. I remember that they had their names on tags in indelible pencil. Dad continued to dig them up every year then plant them again next season. He grew beautiful dahlias.

Next came his interest in Iceland poppies. 'A fellow at work' entered competitions and gave Dad some seeds. It was not long before Dad too was growing 'championship' poppies. Incidentally, I don't think Dad went to a garden nursery in his life; his seeds and plants were always 'from a fellow at work', and Dad was generous with his seeds and plants for fellow gardeners. It was the norm in the 1930s; in fact, I don't remember ever seeing a plant nursery. They came later.

Then Dad grew white chrysanthemums along the fence in the front yard. They were such a beautiful display that people going past wanted to buy a bunch, especially on Mother's Day. So, Dad sold them for two shillings a bunch. There was a steady stream of customers through the weekend. Dad was pleased that his efforts were appreciated.

Dad continued gardening well into his retirement, but gradually became too old, and the backyard at Number 26 took on a sad look as the gardens were neglected. Besides his gardening interests, my father loved singing. He was in Colin Chapman's choir. Colin Chapman was a well-known musician in Newcastle who produced several musical shows. I remember Dad taking the family to see *The Desert Song*, and later *The New Moon*, both produced by Colin Chapman.

A few things come to mind when we were living at Islington that were different to Tighes Hill. I remember that the Co-Op had grocery deliveries. The delivery man knocked on the back door and called out, 'Grocer!' Mum let him in and he sat on a chair in the kitchen and placed his order book on the table. Mum read out her order and he wrote it down. About a week later, there was a call at the back door, 'Grocer!' Mum opened the door and he briskly walked in, placing a box on the kitchen table. One by one the items were quickly stacked in a heap on the table. He put the docket on top and said a cheery, 'Goodbye'. How convenient! Mum paid her Co-op bill at the office in town.

The milkman ran down the side path and filled the enamel jug in the milk box attached to the lattice gate. No money was left out then: it went on the Co-Op account. How things have changed.

I remember the gutter sweeper. Every Friday morning a young man went past our house sweeping the gutter with a very big birch broom. Yes, all the suburban gutters were swept in the late 1930s. I also remember that we did not have to put out the garbage tin as we do now. The garbage man came right around the back and collected it from where it normally stood, emptied it, and placed it back where it was originally standing. What a service!

Another custom sticks in my mind: housewives cleaned their glass windows with screwed up newspaper and methylated spirits.

We always struggled to fit a hose on a tap. The only

Chapter 11 Winding up the 1930s

connection available was a rubber-lined, cast-brass half dome that was tied to the tap with a leather cord. It always squirted in all directions. Threaded taps weren't common until the 1940s.

We really enjoyed living in our new house, and all was right with the world. Then came earth-shattering news. In September 1939, Australians sat in front of their radios in silence to hear Robert Menzies' terrifying words; '... because Great Britain has declared war upon Germany, (pause) ... Australia is also at war ...' I was twelve.

Those words sent shock waves through the nation. I can remember my family, like every other family in Australia just sitting in stony silence, staring ahead, fearful of what would happen next.

Then when Japan came into the war, we were suddenly aware of troop movements. There were road convoys of military vehicles along our highways, seemingly in both directions. We lived near the main railway line and we could see long goods trains loaded with army tanks.

Petrol rationing was the first announcement. Dad's monthly allocation for petrol for the Harley was so small that he said it was not worth paying the registration, so he stood the motorbike on blocks for the duration of the war. There were charcoal burners fitted to the backs of cars, and some had a huge gasbag on top of the car or lorry that flapped going along as it contained less gas.

Then came food rationing with coupon books for tea and clothes. We had to fit blackout curtains and glue tape to the glass windows. It was not long before every shop in Hunter Street had boarded windows. Street lights were fitted with cones that sent a pool of light at the base, and car headlights were covered, allowing only restricted light through slots. We called it the 'brown out'.

At night, searchlight beams probed the night sky and we had practice air raids with complete blackouts. They were worrying times.

So, looking back at the 1930s, the global economic crisis was felt in Australia, just as it was throughout the rest of the world, but we struggled through it. This decade in the history of Australia, including Newcastle, needs to be recorded for future generations. I have attempted to do this by telling my family's story, and in doing so, keep the 1930s alive.

EPILOGUE

My father saw vast changes in his lifetime. Being born in 1901, he was alive when the first aeroplane flight occurred in 1903 and he was still alive when man landed on the moon in 1969. What progress in one lifetime!

In my lifetime, I saw Charles Kingsford Smith's plane, which was the first aeroplane to cross the Pacific Ocean, and I recently heard on the news that a spaceship has set off on an eight-year journey to a distant planet. Also, commercial aeroplanes now carry hundreds of passengers around the world at a time. It is truly amazing to look at the changes in everyday life now compared with the 1930s.

I remember waiting hours at a Sydney suburban post office to be connected to a trunk phone call to Port Macquarie as late as 1954, and now anyone with a mobile phone can call England, or anywhere in the world, instantly. That same small mobile phone can access more information than a set of twenty-six volumes of Encyclopaedia Britannica.

While I marvel at the progress, the world is a different place. In this modern age, I see men marrying men, women marrying women, girls turning into boys and boys turning into girls, couples having a family and then getting married, or not, single mothers everywhere; situations that would be unheard of in the 1930s! This present generation has given us not a 'brave new world' but a 'strange new world'; or so it seems to a Methodist Sunday School boy from the 1930s.

What happened to that working-class boy who grew up in Newcastle in the 1930s? Like every other boy at that time, I saw unemployment everywhere, so I worked hard at school to get a good job. I gained six As and a B in the Intermediate Certificate and three As and three Bs in the Leaving Certificate. An A was over seventy-five per cent and a B was over fifty per cent. Because I liked Technical Drawing at school, I wanted to be a Tech. Drawing teacher, but there were no courses available in 1945, so I commenced an engineering traineeship at Newcastle BHP steelworks. While I was at the steelworks, World War II ended. I will describe it for you because there are not many people still alive today who could give an eye-witness account.

It was an ordinary morning when suddenly at about 10 am on the 2nd of September 1945, all the BHP whistles started blowing continuously, some with short blasts. The foreman of our machine shop must have had a phone call because he ran from one bench to the next yelling, 'The war is over! Take the day off! There are lorries at the front gate!'

Hundreds of BHP employees poured through the gates and jumped onto the lorries. We were taken to central Newcastle where we joined a procession of similarly packed vehicles slowly moving along Hunter Street. There were thousands and thousands of people coming together along the full length of Hunter Street. They were yelling and cheering wildly, waving their arms, and jumping up and down. It was a sight of mass hysteria that I have never seen before or since! Shredded paper was coming from the upper-storey windows like snow, until it was knee-deep on the ground in most places! Music was blaring loudly from all directions and people were holding hands and dancing in circles. Perfect strangers were hugging each other and laughing uncontrollably. This went on for hours! The men on the BHP lorries cheered and added to the noise.

In the afternoon, the lorries took us back to the BHP. I retrieved my bike and rode home; after tea I went back to town. I had recently joined a teenagers' social group of combined YMCA and YWCA members, called the YY Club. Even without mobile phones in those days, we just guessed that everyone would be meeting at the YMCA, and they did. We linked arms and marched up and down Hunter Street. Then we formed a circle and sang, 'The Hokey Pokey,' seemingly hundreds of times until we were all so hoarse, we could hardly speak. At midnight when I left, the party was still going. Incidentally, trams and buses were running but the rides were free! Newcastle was celebrating. It was a day that I shall never forget.

In 1951, Sydney Teachers' College offered an Industrial Arts Diploma course, so I applied and was granted a four-year, full-time scholarship to become an Industrial Arts teacher. After I graduated from teachers' college, I married Gwen Peters, a college student who became a Home Science teacher.

We both taught at Port Macquarie and our children, two daughters and a son, were born at Port Macquarie. Like my mother, I bought land and built a house very early in married life. We enjoyed our time at Port Macquarie, including being foundation members of the newly formed Historical Society and I was president of Apex, a young men's service club.

After ten years at Port Macquarie High School, I was promoted to subject master and appointed to Cowra High School. We had an interesting seven years in mid-western New South Wales, going on many caravan trips with our young family. I then gained the deputy principal position and was appointed to Finley High School in the Riverina, eleven miles from the Murray River. It was a large school with over a thousand students because at that time it was in a rice-growing area with a high concentration of farmers. After seven years as deputy principal, I passed promotion inspection and gained principal status. I elected to remain at Finley High School as principal for a further six years.

With accumulated seniority, I was able to apply for the principal's position of Port Macquarie High School, and I returned to the same school where I had been a junior teacher. I stayed there until I retired and I have remained in Port Macquarie in retirement.

I joined the Lions Club in Finley and transferred membership to the Port Macquarie club when we moved back there. I was president of the Lions Club five times and was awarded the Melvin Jones Fellowship before I retired after forty-six years in the Lions. Probably because of my work with the Lions, I was awarded Hastings District Citizen of the Year in 2010.

Early in retirement, I joined a Thursday bushwalking group. About twenty like-minded retirees walked fifteen to twenty kilometres each Thursday in the hills around Port Macquarie. After a few years, the leader retired so I volunteered to be leader, and led the group for the next ten years. I think it was this period of my life that contributed most to my physical fitness.

In 1993, an advertisement appeared in the local paper for a John Oxley Weekend at Mount Seaview Resort to celebrate 175 years since the explorer John Oxley named Mount Seaview in 1818, so Gwen and I attended. The manager, Ralph Clissold, took the group to the top of Mount Seaview where he read a passage from John Oxley's diary that was written while Oxley and his party were on Mount Seaview. I was so impressed that I decided to follow the whole of John Oxley's 1818 trip from Bathurst to Port Macquarie by car, using a copy of Oxley's diary as a guide. I read his descriptions at the places where they were written and videoed scenes without fences or houses, just as Oxley would have seen them. When I edited the video and showed friends, one friend, Barry Jennings, said that I had not included Beckett's Cataract. I replied that nobody knew where Beckett's Cataract, a waterfall named by John Oxley, was located. Barry said, 'Let's find it.'

After a good deal of research, and receiving permission from property owners, we set out to rediscover Beckett's Cataract. We knew from the diary that it was close to the

Apsley Gorge, south of Walcha, so we drove as close as we could, then walked south until we were on the rim of the Apsley Gorge.

John Oxley wrote in his diary that his progress was stopped by the gorge and that he had to follow the rim of the gorge in a westerly direction. We did the same and discovered a smaller gorge entering the main one. We followed this and found a waterfall that exactly fitted Oxley's description of Beckett's Cataract. I videoed it and edited it into my original video.

Our discovery filled the front page of the local paper and we were regarded as heroes. The Historical Society recommended me for an award for my contribution to local history and the president drove me to Parliament House where I was presented with a NSW Government Heritage Volunteer award by The Hon. Diane Beamer in 2003. My video of the route of Oxley's 1818 trip was shown on a video screen at the Port Macquarie Museum for twelve months.

To celebrate my ninetieth birthday, I hired a bus and took my Thursday bushwalking group to Point Plomer, north of Port Macquarie. We walked along the fifteen-kilometre beach back to Port Macquarie to where our cars were parked at Settlement Point Reserve. Our photograph was printed in the local paper.

I was confident that I could do it because I had walked twenty kilometres along Lighthouse Beach to Lake Cathie and back with my daughter the day before.

My writing began as a regular contributor to the magazine,

Caravan World, after I wrote an article describing a Mini Moke trip to the tip of Cape York, which I had done with my son in 1987. Later, I described our travels through the United Kingdom by car. I also wrote a weekly history column in our local paper, the *Port Macquarie Independent*, for over a year. My first book was *I went with John Oxley*, which is based on his 1818 trip, followed by *Port Macquarie 1821,* celebrating the bicentenary of the town. My most recent book is *Harriet's Boy*, the story of a convict who became a millionaire.

I look back over an interesting life with no regrets; a life that was the result of values, attitudes and ambitions formed while growing up in the 1930s in Newcastle, New South Wales.

www.ingramcontent.com/pod-product-compliance
Lightning Source LLC
Chambersburg PA
CBHW030035100526
44590CB00011B/219